D1544546

Primary Sources of World Cultures™

SPAIN

A PRIMARY SOURCE CULTURAL GUIDE

Graham Faiella

The Rosen Publishing Group's
PowerPlus Books™
New York

Published in 2004 by The Rosen Publishing Group, Inc.
29 East 21st Street, New York, NY 10010

Library of Congress Cataloging-in-Publication Data

Faiella, Graham.
Spain: a primary source cultural guide/ by Graham Faiella.— 1st ed.
    p. cm. — (Primary sources of world cultures)
Summary: An overview of the history and culture of Spain and its people, including the geography, myths, arts, daily life, education, industry, and government, with illustrations from primary source documents.
Includes bibliographical references and index.
ISBN 0-8239-4002-0 (library binding)
1. Spain—Juvenile literature. [1. Spain.] I. Title. II. Series.
DP17.F35 2004
946—dc21

2003003798

Manufactured in the United States of America

Cover images: *The Portal of Love*, Antoni Gaudí's unfinished masterpiece (Templo de la Sagrada Familia), Barcelona *(left)*; title page from the first edition of *Don Quixote* by Miguel de Cervantes *(background)*; Galician dancers in Santiago de Compostela, Spain *(right)*.

Photo credits: cover (background), pp. 20, 24, 25 (bottom), 37, 49, 60, 70, 79, 80, 83 © Archivo Iconografico, S.A./Corbis; cover (middle), 5 (top), 15, 90 © Macduff Everton/Corbis; cover (bottom), p. 56 (bottom) © Nik Wheeler/Corbis; pp. 3, 118, 120 © 2002 GeoAtlas; pp. 4 (top), 8 © Hubert Stadler/Corbis; pp. 4 (middle), 16, 18 © Yann Arthus-Bertrand; pp. 4 (bottom), 38 © Kristi J. Black/Corbis; pp. 5 (middle), 101, 106 © Viesti Collection; pp. 5 (bottom), 108 © Annebicque Bernard/Corbis Sygma; p. 6 © Paul Almasy/Corbis; pp. 7, 87, 88 © Owen Franken/ Corbis; p. 9 © Horacek/Bilderberg/Aurora Photos; p. 10, 30 (top and bottom) © Getty Images; pp. 11, 44 © Michael Busselle/Corbis; p. 12 © Miquel Gonzalez/Laif/Aurora Photos; pp. 13, 72 © Photo Researchers, Inc.; pp. 14, 36, 94 (bottom) © Stuart Cohen/The Image Works; p. 17 © Richard Klune/Corbis; pp. 21, 103 © National Geographic; pp. 22, 71 © AKG; p. 25 (top), 27, 28 (top), 29, 31 (top and bottom), 45, 63, 69, 75 © Art Resource; p. 28 (bottom), 41, 50, 51, 61, 62, 74, 78, 118 (inset) © Bridgeman Art Library; p. 32 (top) © Hulton-Deutsch Collection/ Corbis; pp. 32 (bottom), 64 © Mary Evans Picture Library; pp. 33, 76 (top) © 2003 Estate of Pablo Picasso/Artists Rights Society (ARS), New York; pp. 34, 40, 65, 66, 68, 81 © Corbis; p. 35 © David Wells/The Image Works; p. 39 © David Turnley/Corbis; p. 42 © Pavlovsky Jacques/ Corbis; p. 48 © Dagli Orti/Corbis; p. 52 © Jose Fuste Raga/Corbis; p. 53 © Bilderberg/Aurora Photos; p. 54, 84 (top) © AFP/Corbis; p. 55 (top) © Joanna B. Pinneo/Aurora Photos; p. 55 (bottom) © Hideo Haga/HAGA/The Image Works; p. 56 (top) © Yeshiro Haga/HAGA/The Image Works; p. 57 © Patrick Ward/Corbis; p. 58 © Reuters NewMedia, Inc./Corbis; p. 59 © Abilio Lope/Corbis; p. 76 (bottom) © 2003 Salvador Dali, Gala-Salvador Dali Foundation/Artists Rights Society (ARS), New York; p. 77 © SuperStock; p. 82, 85 © Bettmann/Corbis; pp. 84 (bottom), 98, 110 © Matton Images; pp. 86, 104 © Woodfin Camp & Associates; pp. 89, 92, 96 © Larry Mangino/The Image Works; p. 91 © Vittoriano Rastelli/Corbis; p. 93 © Schultheiss/Bilderberg/Aurora Photos; p. 94 (top) © Jeff Greenberg/The Image Works; p. 95 © The Image Bank/Getty Images; p. 97 © Viesti Collection; pp. 99, 100, 105, 107 © D. Donne Bryant; p. 102 © Joel Azel/Aurora Photos; p. 111 © Peter Arnold; p. 116 © Giraudon/Art Resource.

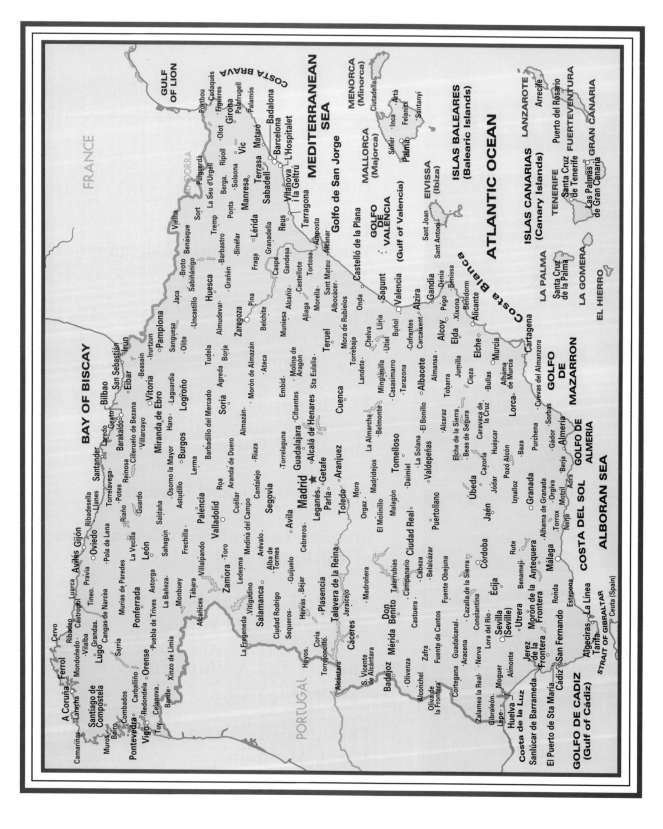

CONTENTS

INTRODUCTION

S pain: the land of castles and churches, bullfights and flamenco, dusty landscapes and blazing heat. Spain is also home to a rich cultural heritage. The
culture of Spain stretches back into prehistory, to the Iberian tribes who populated the land 15,000 years before the birth of Christ and gave their name to what
we know today as the Iberian Peninsula. From the Stone Age paintings in the caves
of the north coast to the surrealist twentieth-century art of Salvador Dalí, Spanish
culture embraces almost twenty millennia. Tribal influences of Visigoths and

Vandals remain. Imperial Roman occupation
lasted 500 years. Almost 800 years of Islamic
domination influenced the architecture, art, and
language of Spain. Spanish imperialism in the
last 500 years sowed the seeds of New World culture in Latin America. Historic architectural
treasures include the Alhambra, the cathedral of
Santiago de Compostela, and Roman aqueducts.
In more recent history, master painters such as
Velázquez, Goya, and Picasso were born in
Spain. Spain has also given the world towering
literary figures including Cervantes, Lope de
Vega, and García Lorca.

And yet, for all this, Spain has existed as a single country only since the
beginning of the sixteenth century. The union of the kingdoms of Castile and

Aerial view of La Gran Vía, the main street of Madrid *(left)*. At the center of the Iberian Peninsula, Madrid
has been the capital of Spain since 1562. Because the city is within relatively easy reach of the other
regions of the country, Madrid has been the connecting point to the rest of Spain. Most of the country's
olive groves are in Andalusia *(above)*. While Spain ranks as the number one producer of olive oil in the
world, this region has the highest unemployment rate in Spain. Because of Andalusia's dependence on
agriculture to support the local economy, climate and drought directly affect jobs.

Spanish writer Miguel de Cervantes' novel *Don Quixote* takes place among the windmills of La Mancha. The best restored windmills can be found just outside the town of Consuegra, in the province of La Mancha in central Spain. A popular energy source in Europe from the late twelfth century until the late eighteenth century, windmills were considered works of art, as no two were alike.

Aragon, after the marriage of Queen Isabella and King Ferdinand in 1469, gradually led to the unification of all the disparate kingdoms of Spain into a single nation. Spain today is a conglomerate of seventeen different political regions. It combines the still dusty plains of Castile and La Mancha with the emerald green mountains and valleys of the north coast. The rugged terrain of Extremadura in the southwest was the birthplace of the conquistadors. The diverse landscapes of Andalusia are home to vineyards, olive groves, and the fighting bulls of the corrida. The off-shore Canary Islands in the Atlantic and Balearic Islands in the Mediterranean attract millions of tourists every year.

The diversity of the regions that characterized Spain's long history before nation-hood is today an orchestra of different instruments, different voices, and even different languages, each playing their part in the symphony that is Spain.

Cut off for centuries from the rest of Europe, invaded countless times, ruled for forty years by one of the twentieth century's most ruthless dictators, Spain was once

The Alcázar in Segovia, at the junction of the Eresma and Clamores Rivers, is part palace and part military fortress. Construction was begun in the late eleventh century by King Alfonso VI on a site once occupied by Romans, Visigoths, and Moors. In addition to its spectacular architecture, the castle has many underground levels and secret passages leading to the rivers and nearby palaces.

the "poor man of Europe." Since the death of dictator Francisco Franco in 1975, it has been catching up with the rest of Europe, to become one of the most enthusiastic partners in the European Union. The Spanish people bring to that partnership a proud cultural heritage as well as a distinct temperament, lifestyle, and vision, born of a long history and economic hardship. Their cave-painting ancestors of so many generations ago left their unique mark on the cultural heritage of Spain. The progression of that lineage is today in the hands of a Europeanized Spanish people who will be challenged to preserve their uniqueness.

THE LAND

The Geography and Environment of Spain

S pain is the second largest country in Europe, by area, after France. It has a total land area of 195,000 square miles (312,000 square kilometers). It is smaller than Texas but bigger than California. It shares the Iberian Peninsula with Portugal (35,500 square miles [56,800 square kilometers]), which occupies most of the west coast. Two island groups also belong to Spain, the Balearic Islands in the Mediterranean and the Canary Islands in the Atlantic. Spain also owns two territories in North Africa: Ceuta and Melilla.

The average height above sea level of the land area of Spain is greater than that of any other country in Europe except Switzerland. Madrid, Spain's capital, is located on the Meseta Central (interior plateau) at the geographic center of the country. Perched at 2,100 feet (635 meters), it is one of the highest capital cities in Europe. The high altitude of the Meseta gives the air a brightness and clarity of light that inspired the quality of Spain's great master painters.

Spain is divided into three parts: peninsular Spain (the mainland), the islands (the Balearic and Canary Islands), and the North African territories of Ceuta and Melilla. About 95 percent of the land area of Spain is the mainland itself.

The Spanish Pyrenees mountains in Aragon *(left)* provide a natural border between France and Spain, separating the Iberian Peninsula from the rest of Europe. The Pyrenean region has three sections, each with its own terrain. The Aragonese section is rugged, the Navarre area is known for its sloping valleys, and the Catalonian section is the most fertile. Olive trees *(above)* thrive in southern Spain, near the Mediterranean coast, where they grow on huge estates. Olives for oil are harvested between September and November.

View of Andalusia with the Strait of Gibraltar and the coast of North Africa in the background. In AD 711, Moors from North Africa crossed the strait and invaded southern Spain. Today, Andalusia is the largest and most populous region of Spain. The Islamic influence remains strong in the region's architecture, language, food, and music.

If you were flying in an airplane over the country from France, you could look down on the Pyrenees mountains. These mountains provide a border between mainland Spain and France, as well as between Spain and the rest of continental Europe. The Pyrenees stretch 248 miles (397 km) across the northeast of Spain. At one end is the Bay of Biscay on the Atlantic side. The Mediterranean is on the other end, to the east and south. Many times in Spain's history, the Pyrenees have served as a wall, isolating Spain from the rest of Europe. The highest peak, Aneto, is 11,169 feet (3,400 m). That's more than two miles high!

You reach the Mediterranean end of the Pyrenees, then turn and cruise down the east coast of Spain, along the Mediterranean Sea. This coast is one of the world's greatest tourist destinations. Each part of the coastline has a different name. The coastal strip from the French border to Barcelona, for example, is called the Costa Brava (wild coast). The Costa Dorada (gold coast) lies between Barcelona and Tarragona, the next big city to the south. The Costa del Sol (sun coast), near Málaga in the south, is one of Spain's biggest tourist areas.

When the tanker *Prestige* spilled over twenty million gallons of oil off the coast of Galicia in 2002, it created an environmental disaster. The oil slick devastated the local fishing industry, the backbone of the region's economy. Scientists believe that the oil might continue to damage the area's environment and economy for the next twenty years.

As you fly over Tarifa, at the southern tip of Spain, you head toward the border with Portugal. Tarifa is the first town on Spain's Atlantic southern coast. Point Tarifa is the tip of the most southern cape of mainland Europe. It guards the Strait of Gibraltar, which separates the Mediterranean from the Atlantic. In the days of sailing ships, Tarifa officials charged a fee to all ships who passed through the Strait of Gibraltar. This is the derivation of the English word "tariff," meaning "a fee."

Next, fly up the long coast of Portugal. At the seaport of Vigo, you're back over Spain. From there you head around Cape Finisterre, Spain's northwest corner. It was named Finisterre by the Romans. They thought it was the end (*finis*, in Latin) of the world (*terre*, in Latin). The people in this region depend mainly on fishing and agriculture. In November 2002, an oil tanker, the *Prestige*, was wrecked just off the coast. Millions of tons of oil drifted on to the shore. The oil pollution killed a lot of fish, birds, and other marine life. You can still see the effects of this ecological disaster: rocks and beaches covered by the thick blanket of oil. It will take years for the environment here to recover.

Looking down, you can see that all around the coast of Galicia there are inlets of the Atlantic, like fjords. These are the Galician rías. The Rías Altas area is on the northern side of this remote corner of Spain. The Rías Bajas (or Baixas, in the local Galician language) are to the south.

Next, crisscross over the north coast of Spain from Galicia to the French border. Fly from the sea coast, over the mountains, a little way inland, and back over the mountains again to the sea. Way below you will see the rocky coast and the stormy

Bay of Biscay. You will cross over the valleys and peaks of the mountain range called the Cordillera Cantábrica. There are green pastures and foothills, snowcapped peaks, and villages. It looks more like what we imagine Switzerland to be than Spain.

The humid air of the Bay of Biscay rises up the sides of the mountains. It condenses and falls as rain before it reaches the other side. This coast gets more rain than anywhere else in Spain. It is a popular area for hunting, fishing, and hiking.

At the border with France, turn inland to fly over the interior of Spain. The first thing you will notice is that there are hardly any people or towns. The interior of Spain is sparsely populated. The population density is just 203 people per square mile (78 people per sq km). The average population density for Europe is about 650–780 people per square mile (250 to 300 people per sq km). The United States has about 78 people per square mile (30 people per sq km). Most of the Spanish population live in big towns and cities.

Looking down, you'll see that the land is dry and rugged. The center of Spain is the Meseta Central, a high, arid plateau. Surrounding the plateau is more dry and rough terrain to the west and southwest. To the northeast is a more fertile region watered by the Ebro River. The Ebro itself is not a big river. The smaller streams that run off the river, however, irrigate a large area. This is known as the Ebro River drainage system. It makes the whole region one of the most agriculturally rich in all of Spain.

Let's head down toward Andalusia in the south. The landscape here varies from rich farmland, to almost desert, to mountain ranges. In some places it looks so much like the Wild West of the United States that a number

A shepherd with his flock in Andalusia. With its warm, sunny climate, Andalusia is known as Spain's southern garden. Sheep farming is one of the most important agricultural industries in the region. Used primarily for wool, milk, and cheese, farm-raised sheep also supplement the country's demand for meat.

Casares, a popular town in Andalusia, is home to about 3,000 people. Although modern life has developed around it, the town retains its ancient flavor. Local legend says that Julius Caesar founded Casares in gratitude for regaining his health at the sulfur springs of nearby La Hediona.

of western movies have been filmed here. Down below we can see a patchwork quilt landscape. There are mountains and valleys (including Spain's most popular ski resorts), large estates of olive trees and vineyards, and small farms. Some of the farms are used to raise bulls for bullfighting.

We'll cross up to the west now. This is the region of Extremadura along the border with Portugal. The landscape is the harshest in Spain: rocky, bare, and dry. This is the home of many of the conquistadors who conquered the Incas and the Aztecs in South America in the fifteenth century. They wanted to escape the poverty of Extremadura (which means, literally, "extremely hard" in Spanish).

So, now you've flown over most of Spain. You have seen mostly a dry country, except for the far north. You have seen some of the tallest mountains in Europe and the fertile plains of the east and south. You have seen a few big cities, some smaller towns, and the tourist resorts of the Mediterranean coast. Now there are two more places to go in Spain: the islands. Let's set down and find a boat!

The Balearic Islands

The first islands we reach are the Balearics. These are between 50 and 190 miles (80–300 km) off Spain's east coast, in the Mediterranean. Our first stop is Majorca (also spelled Mallorca). Then we'll sail over to Ibiza (Iviza, in the Catalan language of the Balearics), and finally to Minorca (Menorca). The small island of Formentera lies just off the coast of Ibiza. Between Ibiza and Majorca is the small uninhabited archipelago of Cabrera. An archipelago is a group of islands. The total land area of the Balearic archipelago is 1,936 square miles (5,014 sq km).

On the island of Ibiza, the Old Town of the city of Ibiza features three world heritage archaeological sites. Phoenician ruins reflect Ibiza's life as a center of Mediterranean commerce around 650 BC. Ibiza's Upper Town retains preserved walls of the early Phoenician settlements incorporated with defensive walls constructed by Arabs and, later, Catalans. Sixteenth-century fortifications are excellent examples of Renaissance military architecture. Beaches and scenery also make Ibiza a popular tourist destination.

The Balearics are famous tourist islands. About one-third of all foreign tourist visitors to Spain head for the Balearic Islands. The largest island in the group, Majorca, is about 3,640 square miles (9,428 sq km). Its landscape varies from mountains, some more than 4,000 feet, to valleys, cliffs and gorges, terraced foothills, pine forests, and some coastal cliffs more than 1,000 feet high. At the center of the island, farmers grow apricots, oranges, figs, and olives, as well as cereal crops such as wheat and alfalfa. Majorca also has some traditional manufacturing industries, including ceramics, pottery, glassware, and footwear.

Each year, more than six million tourists visit Majorca, the biggest island in the Balearic archipelago. An active tourist site since the 1920s, Majorca is home to a lively arts community.

Palma (or Palma de Majorca) is the capital of the Balearic Islands. It is one of the most attractive port cities in all of Spain. Situated on the southwest coast, it is at the center of the ten-mile-wide arc of Palma Bay. After conquering the city in 1229, King Jaime I of Aragon described it as "the most beautiful city I've ever seen." One of its most elegant buildings is the Gothic cathedral, known as Sa Seu to Majorcans. There are many historic buildings throughout the city.

From Palma we sail 50 miles to reach Ibiza to the southwest. Ibiza is 221 square miles (572 sq km). It attracts large numbers of foreign tourists, especially from northern Europe. Like Majorca, but on a smaller scale, the island has mountains (the highest being La Talaya, at 1,558 feet/475 meters), high cliffs, and coves along the rugged north coast. There is small-scale farming. Ibiza's beaches are mainly on the west coast. In the 1960s, many young people came to Ibiza looking for an alternative lifestyle. By the 1980s, mass-market tourism began to take over. Today Ibiza remains largely unspoiled. Just a few places have popular crowded resorts. The resident population of Ibiza is around 60,000.

We sail back to the northeast to reach Minorca, just past Majorca. This quiet little island is about the same size as Ibiza. Its tourism is far less developed, but it is expanding. Walking around a bit, we see the island's landscape is arid and rather monotonous. The coast, however, has a lot of small coves, rocky cliffs, and stretches of beach. Among other products, cereals, figs, potatoes, melons, and

An aerial view of Pico del Teide in Tenerife. From sea level, it takes three days to hike to Spain's highest peak. Most people opt to begin from the crater of Las Cañadas to reach the peak more quickly. Tourists can travel in a cable car most of the way to the top. Tenerife has been called the "island of eternal springtime" because of its temperate climate and lush scenery. The largest of the Canary Islands, Tenerife's economy is based on tourism, the fishing industry, and banana and tomato cultivation.

almonds are produced on the farmlands. Windmills are a typical sight on Minorca. These are used to draw water from artesian wells for irrigation. The capital of Minorca is Mahon. Mayonnaise is named after Mahon! From Mahon, we sail out of the Mediterranean and into the Atlantic to reach Spain's other archipelago: the Canary Islands.

The Canary Islands

The first we see of the Canary Islands is the mountain peak called Teide. It is more than 12,000 feet high (3,658 m) and visible from 80 miles (128 km) away. The Canary Islands lie just off the southernmost coast of Morocco. Fuerteventura is the closest island to the Moroccan coast, just 67 miles (100 km) away. The population of the Canaries is 1.5 million people. The main islands are Lanzarote, Fuerteventura, Tenerife, Gran Canaria, Gomera, La Palma, and Hierro.

Mount Teide, on Tenerife, is 12,198 feet (3,718 m), the highest point on Spanish territory. The Canaries have a subtropical climate. The average temperature is 80° Fahrenheit (26.7° Celsius) in midsummer and about 70°F (21.1°C) in winter. Rainfall generally is about ten inches a year. It rises to thirty inches a year on the rainy windward sides of the islands.

Many people think that the Canaries are named after the birds, canaries. In fact, a Roman writer and historian, Pliny the Elder (AD 23–79), wrote that the Canaries were "so called because of the multitude there of large dogs [*canes*, in Latin]."

On the island of Gomera there is a unique means of communication, the *silbo* ("whistling") language. The native inhabitants, the *guanches*, communicated across the wide valleys of the island by whistling to each other. Gomera is also famous for being the last place where Christopher Columbus stopped before making his first voyage across the Atlantic in 1492.

> ## Tourists like the Canaries
>
> Since the middle of the twentieth century, tourism has become the biggest industry in the Canaries. The subtropical location attracts northern visitors all year round. The main tourist islands are Tenerife, Lanzarote, Gran Canaria, and Fuerteventura. Gomera, La Palma, and Hierro are much less tourist-oriented.

Ceuta and Melilla

On our sail back to mainland Spain, let's stop off at Ceuta and Melilla. These are two small Spanish territories on the Mediterranean coast of Morocco. Ceuta was given to Spain as part of the Treaty of Lisbon in 1688. This port city overlooks the Strait of Gibraltar, the busy shipping channel that connects the Mediterranean Sea and the Atlantic Ocean. Farther east along the coast, Melilla was taken over by Spain in 1497. It is now an important Spanish military post. In 1995, Ceuta and Melilla together, became one of Spain's seventeen autonomous regions.

THE PEOPLE

2

The Ancient Iberians and the Modern Spanish

Early forms of humans inhabited Spain at least 700,000 years ago. Archaeologists have found primitive tools in central Spain dating back at least that far. The earliest human bones that have been found in caves in central Spain date to 280,000 to 300,000 years ago. These early humans, *Homo sapiens*, hunted and made fire. Skulls and other skeleton fossils of Neanderthals, a form of humans that died out around 35,000 years ago, have been discovered in a dozen places around Spain.

Modern humans (*Homo sapiens sapiens*), from 35,000 to 10,000 years ago, gradually developed a more sophisticated culture. They made more specialized flint tools, bone tools, and ornaments. They used needles to sew fur clothes. They were the first people in Spain to make art. Their art is still visible on the walls and ceilings of caves along the north coast. The Cuevas de Altamira, near the town of Santillana del Mar, are the best known of these cave art sites. The people of that time painted the animals they hunted, such as ibex (mountain goat), red deer, reindeer, horses, bison, and aurochs (a now extinct kind of ox). Some of the kinds of animals they painted, such as reindeer, mammoths, and woolly rhinoceroses, indicate how much colder the climate was at that time. It also indicates the lifestyle of

A Mesolithic stone lance head found in the Cave of La Riera, Posada, region of Asturias *(left)*. Neanderthals were hunter-gatherer people who inhabited Europe, dying out about 35,000 years ago. Neanderthals created tools with finely trimmed cutting edges, using flint to form edges that were sharper than a steel scalpel. Many Neanderthal tools found in Spain are about 35,000 years old. Above is a crocodile fossil from Las Hoyas.

Altamira is in the mountains of northern Spain. Archaeologists believe that the cave paintings there were created between 16,000 and 9,000 BC by the Magdalenian people. The cave paintings depict bison, hunted by the cave dwellers for the food, skins, bones, and fur they provided. There are fifteen bison images on the ceiling of the cave. Deer and boar are pictured on the walls. Many of the animals were painted on natural rock protrusions, giving them a three-dimensional look.

these people as nomadic, or wandering, hunters who sheltered in caves. The last ice age ended about 12,000 years ago.

These Paleolithic (which means "old stone age") cave paintings suggest that Spain was a cradle of modern European civilization dating back to the ice age. France is the only other country in Europe where there is as much cave art as in Spain. The cold-climate animals that people hunted disappeared after the last ice age. The sea level rose. It flooded land around the coast. People had to travel farther inland to find food. We know about them from the art they left behind in caves and on cliff walls all around Spain. They painted more complicated scenes, such as groups of people hunting, people fighting, people wearing ceremonial clothing and ornaments, and even people climbing ladders to gather honey from beehives. The paintings show how the culture and society of early humans in Spain became more sophisticated. They were still hunting and looking for food around 6000 BC.

Only after that time did they gradually become more settled in larger communities. Eventually these settlements became villages, towns, and cities.

The early inhabitants of northern Spain began to make pottery, grow crops, keep domesticated animals, and live in larger communities from about 5500 BC. This was the Neolithic, or new stone age, period. The Neolithic culture spread south over the next 1,500 years. It reached the inhabitants of southern and southwestern Spain and the area now known as Portugal, between 4500 BC and 3800 BC.

By 3000 BC, there were large settlements of communities around Spain, particularly in the south. Some of the settlements had defenses such as walls and lookout towers. The people mined copper and made simple copper tools. They grew wheat and barley. They raised farm animals. There was tribal warfare among them. They buried their dead in religious ceremonies. There were different social classes within each community.

There were many kinds of tribal settlements. The societies of the different groups became more sophisticated. They began to cultivate more land. In the Bronze Age (about 2000 BC to about 800 BC), there were rich people in some kinds of settlements

Before There Was Spain

It is important to understand that Spain was first simply a land area, the Iberian Peninsula, connected to the rest of the European continent (where there were still no countries, either). People lived in small communities. Groups of communities organized into tribes. A tribe is a group of communities that share a common heritage, culture, identity, and set of ambitions. The strongest tribes in the peninsula dominated other tribes. Spain only became a country—a nation—when the many groups united thousands of years later. The land we now call Spain was, in those early years, simply a large land area populated by different tribes.

who lived apart from the others. There were also different kinds of settlements in different areas: simple fortified settlements called *castros* along the north coast, small farming settlements in the northeast, and isolated fortified villages (*motillas*) on the Meseta Central.

An Iberian sculpture of a female dating from the Iron Age. Inhabiting southern and eastern Spain between the sixth and second centuries BC, the Iberians are believed to have migrated from Africa. Gold hair needles and earrings, glass pendants, and iron farm equipment used by Iberians have been found by archaeologists.

The Iberians and Phoenicians

By around 800 BC, the Bronze Age people inhabiting southern and southeastern Spain had a very distinctive culture. The Greeks, who came to Spain as traders around 800 BC, called these people "Iberians." The name probably comes from the Iberus (now called the Ebro) River, where the Iberians lived. By the time of the Greek historian Herodotus (550 BC), the name "Iberian" referred just to the native people living between the Ebro River in the northeast and the southwest coast. Eventually the whole peninsula of Spain and Portugal came to be called the Iberian Peninsula.

The Iberian civilization was complex. There were independent cities and confederations (groups) of cities. The Iberians knew how to work iron. Their art was sophisticated. The Iberian language was the first native written language in Spain. The alphabet was based on Phoenician writing from around 800 BC. Only a few examples of the Iberian language survive today. These are inscriptions on stone tablets, metal plates, and pottery. Their meanings remain a mystery. No one has yet been able to understand the Iberian language.

Phoenicians came from the areas we know today as Lebanon, Syria, and Israel.

A Phoenician trade ship carved in relief on a sarcophagus. Flourishing between 1200 and 332 BC on the coast of the Mediterranean Sea, Phoenicians were thought to be the best seafaring traders and ship-builders of the ancient world. Known for making purple dye from the murex snail, the word "Phoenician" is Greek for "dealer in purple."

They were in the Mediterranean areas of Spain as early as 1200 BC. They traveled to Spain in search of precious metals and minerals to pay their masters, the Assyrians. The Phoenicians mined silver and gold in southern Spain at the Río Tinto mines. The mines are still worked today. Phoenicians also built Cádiz, on the south coast, around 1100 BC. Cádiz is the oldest continually inhabited city in Europe. The Phoenician empire faded by 550 BC, but Phoenician colonies survived in Spain. They acted as trading posts for the Carthaginians, who became dominant in this part of the Mediterranean.

Romans and Barbarians

The Carthaginians had established outposts along the Spanish Mediterranean coast. These were used mainly as bases from which to fight against Rome to the east. The Roman Empire sent troops to Spain in the year 218 BC to defeat the Carthaginians. "Romanization" of Spain was slow at first. It took 300 years, until

This Iberian lion sculpture from the Iron Age closely resembles the sculpture of other Mediterranean cultures, such as those of ancient Greece and Etruria. During the Iron Age, art shifted from being funerary objects to representing the wealth of the aristocracy.

the time of Julius Caesar, for Roman customs to be fully integrated in Spain. Christianity became established in the second century AD. By the third century AD, the Romans were reducing their military presence in Spain.

In AD 376, the Roman emperor Valens allowed tribes of Visigoths to enter and settle in Spain. The Visigoths were fair-skinned and tall. They came from near the Danube River in central Europe. In AD 410, the Visigoth king Alaric invaded Rome itself. After that, Visigoths and other so-called barbarian tribes, the Suebians, Alans, and Vandals, invaded Spain as Roman rule weakened. These tribes coexisted with the much larger Spanish-Roman population for the next 400 years.

Roman civilization, and Roman law in particular, dominated the culture of tribal Spain during these centuries. The Visigoths converted to Roman Catholicism around AD 600. The Visigothic book of Roman law, *Liber Iudicorum*, written around AD 650, is an important Visigothic legacy of and tribute to Roman influence and power in Spain.

Islamic Spain and the Reconquest

In the year AD 711, an army of Moors (Muslims) from North Africa defeated the Visigoth king Roderick in a battle in southern Spain. Within two years, Muslim forces overran the entire Visigoth kingdom in most of the rest of Spain. The remaining Visigothic Christian populations of Spain gathered in the northern mountains and valleys of Asturias and Galicia. This was the only part of Spain the Muslim invaders never reached.

For the next 800 years, the southern half of Spain was basically Islamic. The northern half was predominantly Christian. Throughout this time, the Christian forces battled against Muslims to regain and unite Spain as a Christian civilization. This struggle was called La Reconquista (the Reconquest). The northern Christian kingdoms were Asturias, Castile, León, Aragon, and Catalonia. The Moors in the south called their territory Al-Andalus. Today this southern part of Spain is called Andalusia.

The Reconquest was a period of advances and retreats by both sides. Muslims sometimes joined forces with Christians. Christians and Muslims fought among themselves. Conflicts between the different Muslim rulers weakened their power. This made it easier for Christian forces to advance. During this period, the Christian

A fresco dating from AD 1229 depicts the conquest of Majorca, with Moors riding out to war. Moors occupied the island of Majorca for five centuries. The island, located in the Mediterranean, was a strategic location at the center of the trade routes between Africa, the Orient, and the Iberian Peninsula. In 1229, Jaime I of Aragon sought to reclaim the island from the Moors. He led the conquest of Majorca in the name of Christianity but ultimately seized the land so his own kingdom would control Mediterranean trade and commerce.

A fresco dating from AD 1229 depicts the conquest of Majorca by Jaime I of Aragon. Once Jaime I reclaimed Majorca, he established his own base for trade. Soon Christian settlers inhabited the island. The last Moors were driven out of Majorca in 1287.

rulers of the northern kingdoms created many of the legal and political institutions that survive in Spain today. Many features of Islamic civilization are also still visible in Spain today. The architecture of many buildings in southern Spain in particular is Islamic. The Spanish language itself contains many words of Arabic origin.

Modern Spain

The 800 years of Islamic rule in Spain ended on January 2, 1492. On that day, the Muslim ruler of Granada, the last Islamic stronghold in Spain, surrendered to Christian forces, enabling Spain to unify into a single country. To this day, it has been ruled by Catholic monarchs in an almost unbroken line.

Ferdinand II, king of Aragon, and Isabella I, queen of Castile, are known in Spain as the Reyes Católicos (Catholic Monarchs"). After they married, they united the two dominant kingdoms in Spain at the time: Castile (most of western Spain) and Aragon (most of eastern Spain). That union

A dish with Arabic inscription dates from the fifteenth century. Arabic is the language of Islam and of the Koran, the Islamic holy book. The Moors, after conquering Spain, established Córdoba. The most sophisticated city in Europe, it was home to 500,000 people and had 60,000 palaces, 70 libraries, 900 public baths, 700 mosques, and Europe's first streetlights.

lead to the birth of Spain as a single unified country. But the birth of the country we know as Spain was not straightforward. Baby España was traumatically induced into being after a long and difficult birth.

Ferdinand and Isabella married in October 1469. Isabella's father, King Henry IV of Castile, died in 1473. The following year, in 1474, Isabella was crowned queen of Castile. That same year, Ferdinand's father, John II, king of Aragon, died. So Ferdinand became king of Aragon. From 1479, Ferdinand and Isabella ruled Castile and Aragon jointly: Isabella as Queen Isabella I of Aragon and Castile, and Ferdinand as King Ferdinand II of Aragon and Ferdinand V of Castile.

Isabella died in 1504. The heir to her throne was one of her daughters, Joan. She was known as Juana la Loca (or Joan the Mad). Joan became queen of Castile in 1504. When Ferdinand died in 1516, she also became queen of Aragon, until her own death in 1555.

Spanish artist Francisco Ortiz Pradilla completed his painting *The Surrender of Granada* between 1879 and 1882. He depicts the Moorish leader, Boadil, handing over the keys of the city to the Catholic Monarchs in 1492. The treaty stated that the language, religion, and customs of the Moors would be respected by the Catholic monarchy. However, subsequent treaties between the Moors and the Catholic Monarchs reduced the Muslim population and their freedom to practice the Islamic religion in Spain.

Queen Isabella and King Ferdinand, as seen in this 1469 painting, were known as the Catholic Monarchs. Their marriage unified the country and strengthened the Catholic Church in Spain. Ruling as equals, they defeated the Portuguese invasion, regained Granada, expelled the Jews and the Moors, established the Spanish Inquisition, and financed the voyage of Christopher Columbus.

Joan was legally queen for fifty years. But she was considered insane and unfit to rule. Ferdinand therefore ruled both Aragon and Castile until 1506. Then Joan's husband, Philip, claimed his right to become King Philip I of Castile in 1506. But he lasted only a month before he died.

Therefore, Ferdinand returned to be the king of Castile as well as of his own kingdom, Aragon. When he died in 1516, his grandson (the son of Philip I and Joan) became King Charles I of Spain. He abdicated (gave up the throne) in 1556. (He was also the Holy Roman Emperor Charles V from 1519 until 1556.)

From the time of the Reyes Católicos, Spain gradually, and with difficulty, became a modern European imperial state. The first voyage of Christopher Columbus,

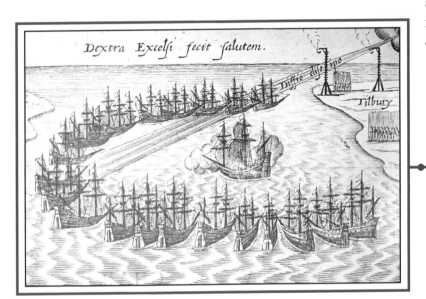

A woodcut depicts the Visigoths, led by Alaric, capturing Rome in AD 410. Originally barbarians from central Europe, the Visigoths evolved into a highly cultured people. Their kingdom encompassed the southern part of Gaul (present-day France) and a large part of Spain. Around 526, the Franks drove them out of Gaul. The Visigoth government seat was moved to Toledo, Spain.

A portrait of Charles I, dated 1532. After preventing the Turks from invading Spanish territory, he was unable to defeat them in the Mediterranean. Initiating wars with France for control of northern Italy, his conquests created debts amounting to one million ducats. To raise money, he increased taxes and sold offices and crown land. The selling of crown land provided revenue but hurt Spain's financial future. The royal salt mines were sold to private owners who were exempt from taxes. In 1556, Charles I abdicated the throne and retired to a monastery.

in 1492, was sponsored by Isabella I. It enabled Spain to extend its imperial reach across the Atlantic to the New World.

In the twentieth century, the Spanish Civil War (1936–1939) was one of the most tragic periods in Spain's history. On July 18, 1936, right-wing forces of the army (the Nationalists) rose up in rebellion to overthrow the government. On the government side (the Republicans), trade unions and left-wing political parties (Communists, Republicans, and Socialists, among others) opposed the Nationalists.

The Nationalists were united under the army. Adolf Hitler of Germany and Benito Mussolini of Italy supplied them with arms. The Soviet Union (Russia) supported the Republicans, sending them arms. Political differences, however, weakened the Republican forces. In 1938, the Soviet Union sent them less weapons. On March 28, 1939, the more unified and better armed Nationalist forces marched into Madrid,

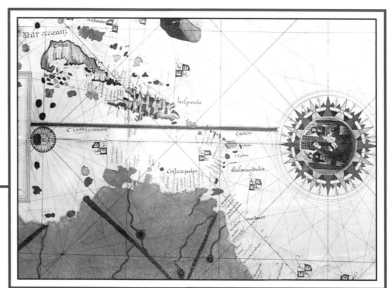

A map from about 1500 by Spanish sea captain Juan de la Cosa, who crossed the Atlantic Ocean thirteen times, including three times with Columbus. His was the first map to show Cuba, Puerto Rico, Jamaica, the Antilles, and the coastline of the American continent.

Republican fighters in northern Spain surrender to Nationalist troops during the Spanish Civil War The Republican government came to power in 1931, advocating land reform and workers' rights. In 1936, it was attacked by the Nationalist forces of General Francisco Franco.

the capital and last Republican stronghold. The Republicans officially surrendered on April 1, 1939.

Francisco Franco (1892–1975) was one of the generals who led the army rebellion that began the civil war. After the Nationalists' victory, he became dictator (*caudillo*) of Spain. His dictatorship lasted more than thirty-five years, until his death on November 20, 1975.

After Franco's death, Spaniards gradually adjusted to democracy and newfound freedoms. A new constitution was signed into law in December 1978. The 1978 constitution guaranteed many civil, religious, and social rights and freedoms that were not allowed during Franco's dictatorship. In 1986, Spain became a member of the European Economic Community (now called the European Union).

Modern Spain has a democratically elected Parliament (Cortes). It consists of a Congress of Deputies (Congreso de los Diputados) and Senate (Senado). It is

General Franco reviewing his troops *(left)*. Appointed generalísimo of Nationalist Spain and head of state after the Spanish Civil War in 1939, Franco was a brutal dictator who employed ruthless means to maintain power. When he died in 1975, in accordance with his request, the monarchy was restored to Prince Juan Carlos. In 1937, Joan Miró created a poster *(right)* titled *Aidez l'Espagne* to support the Republican cause during the Spanish Civil War. Miró used a menacing figure of a peasant from Catalonia, his native region, to represent the Republican defiance.

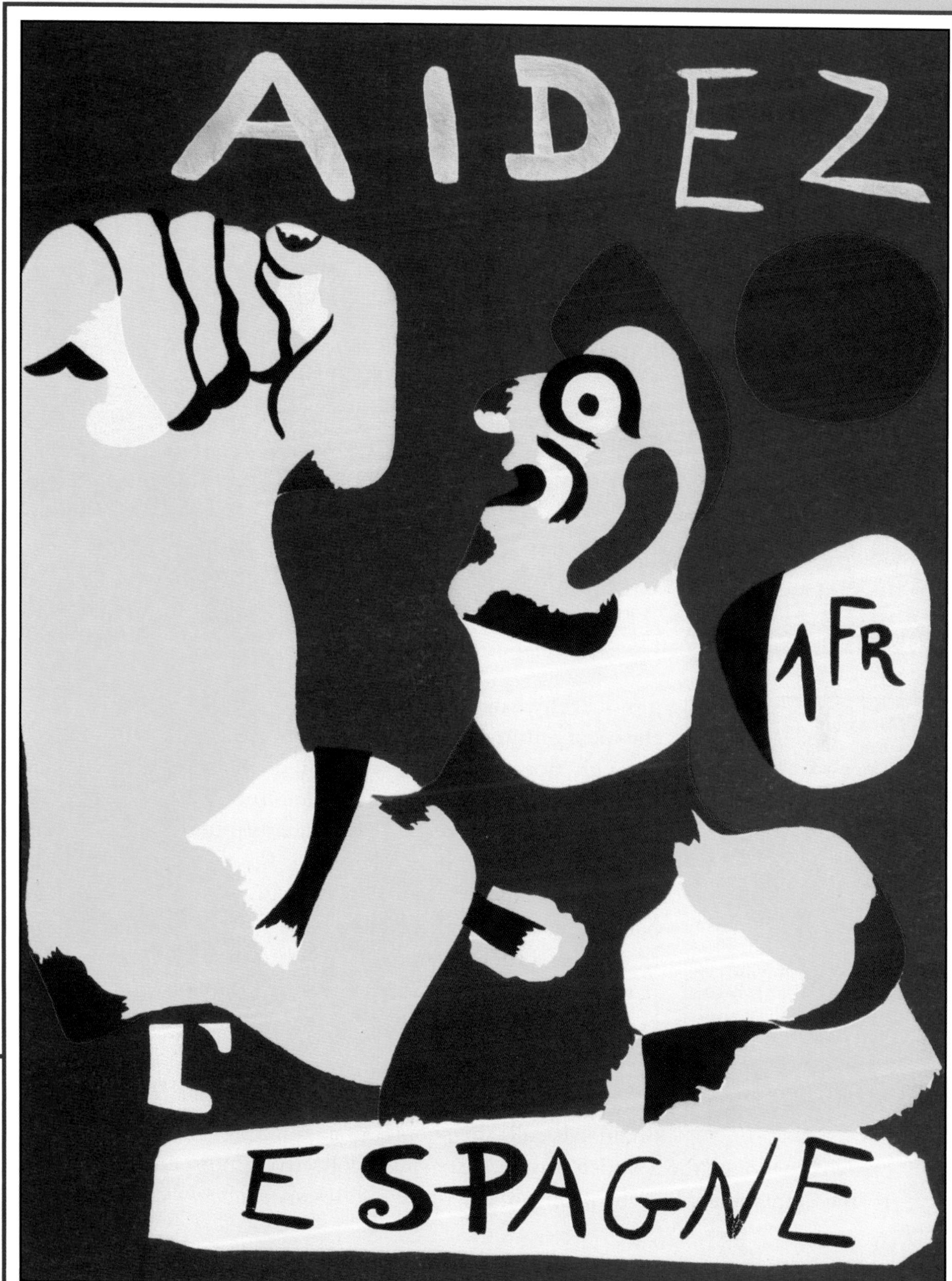
AIDEZ
1 FR
L'
ESPAGNE

a monarchy, currently under King Juan Carlos I. It is one of the most enthusiastic partners of the European Union. Most (though not all) of its regional political differences have been resolved. The biggest problem remaining is the Basque separatist movement ETA, which continues to use terrorism in its struggle to create a separate Basque state.

Spaniards today enjoy a rich, diverse culture that dates back thousands of years. They have a standard of living equal to that of other Mediterranean European countries. They have created a truly Spanish culture out of their common heritage and regional diversity.

El Pueblo Español

Spaniards call "the people" of a country or region *el pueblo*. *El pueblo español* is "the Spanish people," as a single collective group. *El pueblo catalán* is "the Catalan people." The people of the United States are *el pueblo norteamericano*.

The People: The Ancient Iberians and the Modern Spanish

Most Spaniards are Roman Catholic, although Spain's constitution gives every Spaniard the freedom to decide which religion he or she chooses to follow. The Spanish constitution also guarantees human, political, cultural, and linguistic rights of diverse social groups.

They are also called *los españoles*, *los catalanes*, and *los norteamericanos*. But most commonly they are referred to as el pueblo. Any collective group of people, in fact, is el pueblo in Spanish, as in, for example, *la voz del pueblo* ("the voice of the people").

"El pueblo" literally means "the town" in Spanish. It is interesting that this word is used to describe the people in this way. For all their differences, the people are reduced to the concept of the town. Perhaps one reason is because Spaniards have always been a very homogeneous people, meaning that they are racially and culturally very similar. There are very few Spaniards who are not Caucasian (white) and Catholic. Even during the time of Islamic Spain (711 to 1492), most of the population was Caucasian and Christian. Before that, the Romans, Visigoths, and other Germanic tribes were Caucasian.

Fuenteovejuna is a famous play by the great Spanish playwright Lope de Vega. The play, based on real events, takes place in the village of Fuenteovejuna in the time of the Reyes Católicos, Ferdinand and Isabella. In the play, the lord of the village, who is the representative of the king, rapes a village girl. All the villagers get together and kill the lord. The king sends a judge to find out who murdered the lord. The judge asks the villagers who committed the crime. The villagers, even under torture, respond only that *"Fuenteovejuna lo hizo!"* (We all did it!"). The king rewards them for this heroic act of unity by placing them under his protection.

"El pueblo" can mean the town, or village, but also "the people." It is collective force that takes responsibility together for its actions and beliefs. This is perhaps what "el pueblo español" really means to Spaniards as "the Spanish people": many voices of many people, speaking as one voice of the people.

THE LANGUAGES OF SPAIN

3

From Ancient Spanish to Modern Spanish

Everyone knows that in Spain people speak Spanish. But there are actually four different languages spoken in Spain: so-called Castilian Spanish, Catalan, Basque, and Galician (*gallego*, in Spanish). Virtually everyone in Spain knows how to speak Castilian Spanish. Catalan, however, is the first language for around 7 million speakers in the northeast region of Catalonia (Cataluña, in Spanish). There are approximately 520,000 Basque speakers in the Spanish Basque (Euskadi) Country provinces of Guipúzcoa, Vizcaya, Navarre (Navarra, in Spanish), and a small part of Alava along the north coast. (There are another 80,000 or so Basque speakers in the French Basque Country.) Around the northwest corner of Spain and particularly in Galicia, Galician is spoken by an estimated 1.5 million people.

There are also different dialects spoken around Spain, including Galician dialects in the northwest and at least three dialects of Catalan in the northeast and the Balearic Islands. There are seven dialects of the Basque language. The differences between the dialects of Basque, Galician, and Catalan are small enough so that most Basque, Galician, and Catalan speakers can understand each other, whatever their dialectal differences. Finally, there are differences in

A man window-shops at a food store in Madrid (*left*). Spain has one official national language, Spanish, and three co-official languages: Catalan, Basque, and Galician. Catalan is spoken in the regions of Catalonia, Valencia, and the Balearic Islands. Galician is spoken in Galicia, in northwest Spain. Basque (or Euskera as it is called in the Basque language) is unrelated to any known language spoken today. A poster (*above*) dated June 8, 1885, advertises a bullfight in Cádiz.

Posters advertise tango dancing and bullfights. In addition to speech, Spaniards also use body gestures to communicate. Snapping the thumb and second finger is a form of applause. When talking about a person who is considered stingy, or cheap, one taps the left elbow with the right hand. A Spaniard who has heard a story before might put his right hand behind his head and pull his left ear. Men hug when greeting each other. Women greet each other with a hug and a small kiss on both cheeks.

the pronunciation and accents of Castilian Spanish in the different regions of Spain.

Spanish, Catalan, and Galician are called Romance languages. (Other Romance languages are French, Italian, Portuguese, and Romanian.) They derive from Latin. Basque is not related to Latin or any other language spoken in the world today. Basque languages were spoken in southwest Europe before the Roman Empire. The language today has survived in its present form from those pre-Roman times.

The Basques and Catalans are proud of their heritage. The Basque and Catalan languages have been, in different degrees, instruments of their people to express their cultural and political identities distinct from the rest of Spain. Catalan, with Castilian Spanish, is the co-official language of the autonomous region of Catalonia. Basque is the co-official language in the Basque Country autonomous region. Galician has official co-language status in the autonomous region of Galicia.

The Languages of Spain: From Ancient Spanish to Modern Spanish

Spanish is the mother tongue of 332 million people in twenty-one countries. Overall, about 500 million people throughout the world speak Spanish. It is the second most widely used language in international business.

Castilian

The language we know as Castilian today was originally a local dialect of Cantabria, on the north coast. It is called Castilian (*castellano*) because it became the court language of the kingdom of Castile and León in the twelfth century. When the kingdoms of Castile, León, and Aragon merged in the fifteenth century, Castilian became the standard language of all Spain. Now Castilian is the official state language of Spain.

Sometimes the language is called Spanish (*español*). Sometimes it is called Castilian (castellano). It is only called Castilian Spanish in English, never in Spanish. The preferred term generally in Spanish is "castellano." This is because the term "español" refers to both the language and, as an adjective, to the state (España). There is sensitivity to the use of "español" to mean the Spanish language. It suggests superiority over other languages in Spain because it refers also to the state. "Castellano" is therefore the more politically correct term in Spain. The constitution of 1978 refers to the language as castellano.

There are 40 million Spanish speakers in Spain. In Latin America, Spanish-speaking Caribbean islands (Dominican Republic, Cuba, Puerto Rico), and elsewhere around the world, approximately 332 million people speak Spanish as their mother tongue. Among all the world's 2,700 or so different languages, only English and Chinese have more speakers than Spanish.

Spanish is more or less the same language wherever it is spoken, including in Latin America. It is a myth that Latin American Spanish is different from the Castilian version spoken in Spain. The main difference is the pronunciation. In most of Spain, the pronunciation of "c" when it comes before "e" or "i" (*cena, estancia*), and of "z" when it comes before any vowel (*zapato, azul*), is "th." In southern Spain, as well as in the Canary Islands, the "c" and "z" in those circumstances are pronounced "s." The first Spanish explorers and conquerors of Latin America were from southern Spain. They brought that pronunciation of "c" and "z" with them. That is still the main difference between Latin American Spanish and Castilian Spanish to this day.

There are also vocabulary differences in Latin American Spanish. In Spain, for example, a bus is an *autobus*. In parts of Central America it is a *guagua*! In other places (including some parts of Spain) it is a *camión*. In Spain a *camión* is a truck. The urban Hispanic community, originally in New York City, created new words to express the kind of environment they live in. A roof in Spain is *techo*. In apartment buildings of New York City in Hispanic areas, the roof is not only the covering of a house (*techo*), but also a place where people socialize. The Hispanic American Spanish reflects that difference: the roof of an apartment building is called *el roof*! In Spain, also, the concept of an American backyard is uncommon. Most people in Spain live in apartment blocks. A Hispanic American Spanish word for a backyard is therefore *el backyard*.

A number of Spanish words derive from Arabic, from the time of the Islamic occupation of Spain. *Almohada* (pillow), for example, and other nouns beginning with *al*, derive from the Arabic. (*Al* means "the" in Arabic.)

Accents of Spanish differ between the regions of Spain as they do between the countries of Latin America. The "purest" form of Spanish is said to be spoken in the central and northern areas of Spain.

In Andalusia (southern Spain) the accent can be difficult, if not impossible, for outsiders to understand. It is even more difficult because they speak very quickly.

A boy is engrossed in a Basque translation of *The Adventures of Tintin*, created in Belgium by artist Hergé beginning in the early 1940s. Still popular with readers of all ages, Tintin books have been translated into fifty languages. In the Basque version, Tintin is named "Tintinen" and Snowy the dog is called "Milu."

"Open-Air Feast," from a 1554 Arabic book of poems. Laws passed in Spain between 1501 and 1566 banned the use of Arabic, including in books and contracts. While the Moors were expelled from Spain at the end of the fifteenth century, Islamic cultural influences continued to be evident.

Andalusian Spanish speakers do not pronounce the separate letters of words as clearly as in other parts of Spain. Andalusian pronunciation commonly loses the sound of the "s" in the middle and at the end of words. For example, the word *este* ("this") becomes *e'te*, and the word *vamos* ("let's go," "we go") becomes *vamo'*. This is also very common in the accents of Latin America and the Spanish-speaking Caribbean.

Catalan

Catalan is the language of Catalonia in northeast Spain and of the Balearic Islands. Dialects of Catalan are spoken around Valencia, as well as in both Majorca and Ibiza. It is also the official language of Andorra, the tiny country in the Pyrenees mountains between Spain and France. There are also native Catalan speakers in the southern French area of Rousillon and on the Italian island of Sardinia.

Catalan was the official language of the kingdom of Aragon in the twelfth century. The earliest literature written in Catalan dates from that period. When Spain became unified as a country in the fifteenth and sixteenth centuries, Catalan became a minority language in Spain. In recent times, Catalonia has become the most powerful region of Spain. Its language, Catalan, has also grown in importance.

There are many differences between Catalan and Spanish, in grammar, vocabulary, and pronunciation. The simple past tense in Catalan, for example, is formed by combining the present tense of the verb "to go" with the infinitive of the main verb.

Newspapers and magazines written in Basque, or Euskera. In Basque, there are no words for abstract concepts or modern tools and utensils. Instead, the Basque people use a Latin, French, or Spanish word with a Basque ending. Fork, *fourchette* in French, becomes *fourchetta* in Basque.

"I go" (or "I am going") in Catalan is *jo vaig* (pronounced *zho vhatch*). The verb "to walk" is *caminar*. "I walked," in Catalan, is therefore *jo vaig caminar*. (There is also a more formal construction, *jo caminí*, which is more like the Spanish, *yo caminé*.) Catalan also has the "ç," called a cedilla, (as in *cançó*, meaning "song"), which Spanish does not have. Accent marks in Catalan can be either grave (that is, open, as in *pèl*, meaning "hair") or acute (that is, closed, as in *déu*, meaning "god"). Spanish uses only the closed (acute) accent mark. Catalan does not use the Spanish letter "ñ," prounounced en-yay, (as in Cataluña). It uses "ny" to make the "ñ" sound (Catalunya).

Basque

The Basque name for the Basque Country is Euskadi. It comes from the Basque name for the Basque language, *euskera*. Basque has been a language since Neanderthal times 35,000 years ago. The first book written in Basque was *Linguae Vasconum Primitiae*, which appeared in 1545. Before then Basque was mainly a spoken language. From the seventeenth century until the early twentieth century, the Basque language declined as Spanish dominated the country.

In 1914, however, the first *ikastola* was established. ("Ikastola" is the Basque word for a school where all subjects are taught in Basque.) The Royal Academy for the Basque Language (Euzkaltzaindia) was established in 1918. After the Spanish Civil War (1936–1939), Basque was abolished by the dictator General Franco. By the 1960s, however, the language began to revive. More ikastolas were set up. The 1978 constitution gave people the constitutional right to use Basque. Nowadays, the Basque language is an important part of Basque culture. It is taught in bilingual

(Basque and Spanish) schools in the Basque Country. There are Basque-language television and radio stations as well as magazines. The official Basque Country Web site (Euskadi.net) promotes the understanding of Basque culture and language. Outside Spain there are now many Basque cultural centers around the world.

The main grammatical difference between Spanish and Basque is that Basque uses suffixes (parts added on to the end of words) to change the meaning of the word. For example, "house" in Spanish is *casa*. In Basque it is *etxe* (pronounced *etchay*). "The house" in Spanish is *la casa*. In Basque, "the house" is *etxe-a*. Something that belongs to, or is from, the house is *de la casa* in Spanish. In Basque it is *exte-a-ren*. Although most Basque words are completely unrelated to Spanish or other Romance languages, it has borrowed words from Spanish (for example, *arbola*, from the Spanish for "tree," *árbol*).

Famous Basque people include the modern sculptor Eduardo Txillida (Chillida, in Spanish) (1924–); the explorer Juan Sebastián de Elkano (Elcano) (c. 1476–1526), who took command of Ferdinand Magellan's fleet of ships making the first voyage around the world when Magellan was killed in the Philippines; Ignatius de Loyola (1491–1556), who founded the Jesuits; and the golfer José-María Olazabal (1966–).

Galician

Galician (*gallego*) is the ancestor of modern Portuguese. It was the language of the royal court in the fourteenth century. As Spanish came to dominate the country after the unification of Spain in the fifteenth and sixteenth centuries, Galician declined. It was mostly spoken in rural areas and the home. By the nineteenth century, it was associated with poverty and backwardness. There was a temporary revival of the language in the late nineteenth and early twentieth centuries. In 1906, the Academy of the Galician language was established. However, it was not until the 1978 constitution that Galician became an officially recognized regional language.

Galician is very similar to Portuguese. The definite article ("the") is the same as in Portuguese: *a casa* ("the house") in Galician is the same in Portuguese, *a casa* (*la casa*, in Spanish). The word for "street" in Galician is *rua*. This is the same as in Portuguese, but is very different from the Spanish word for "street," *calle*. So, most street names (and signs) in Galicia say *rua*, not *calle*.

SPANISH MYTHS AND LEGENDS

4

Most of the mythology and folklore of Spain is regional. Many myths from Asturias, in the north, for example, relate to water. The region faces the Bay of Biscay, which is often very stormy. It also has many rivers, streams, and mountain springs. It rains in Asturias more than in most other places in Spain. In Asturia, the spirit of the sea is called Espumeru (*espuma* means "foam" or "surf" in Spanish). This childlike spirit dances in the surf breaking against the coast and

against the bows of boats at sea. During storms, Espumeru takes shelter in caves along the cliffs. There are also shy wood nymphs, called xanas. They hide in the forests. Xanas dress in the typical Asturian fashion of red skirts. They comb their blond hair with golden combs.

Some of the mythology of Spain goes back to prehistoric times. The mythology centers around pagan (pre-Christian) gods and goddesses. Some of these are Lug, god of the sun; Tagotis, god of hell and bad luck; Net, god of war; Sitiouio and Poemana, god and goddess, respectively, and protectors of livestock; Durbed, a rather degenerate genie that lives in rivers and lakes; Tameobrigo, a spirit who comforts the sick; Acheóo, a bull-god that symbolizes strength and manhood; and Favonius, god of the winds.

There are mythological creatures for most natural things, such as the wind, sun, sea, forests, and rain. There are creatures of the imagination, too, such as devils and

Coastal cliffs near Gijon, in Spain's Asturias region *(left)*. A painting by Juan Carreño de Miranda *(above)* is titled *Saint James the Great in the Battle of Clavijo*. It depicts Saint James, who, rose from his grave during the Battle of Clavijo in AD 834 to help the Christian army defeat the Moors. Since then, the Spanish have believed in the miraculous power of St. James and call his name in battle.

imps, fairies and angels. These goblins, imps, and spirits, both good and bad, are *duendes* in Spanish. In Spain there are thousands of duendes in the popular myths and stories of all the regions. Most of them are impish: They play jokes on people and generally get into all kinds of mischief. They are mythical creatures that are believed to live among us, as figures of our imagination. Duendes in Spain most commonly live in dark little places, like the corners of old barns, in attics, or under the furniture. In fact, duendes usually refer to household goblins rather than to creatures that live in the countryside. It is said that the word "duende" comes from *duen* (*dueño*) *de casa* (owner of the house). Duendes are small, like tiny children, but with old-looking faces. In the distant past, duendes were often shown as having tails and horns, like little devils.

Around the northeast regions of Aragon and Catalonia and in Majorca, there is a type of duende called a *follet*. These tiny creatures might hide in a horse's mane and make him gallop. They are typically shown as little gnomes with white beards and red berets. Other regions of Spain have their own distinctive kinds of duendes.

There are also national myths and legends of Spain. All Spaniards know them. Many are in the form of poems or short stories. Others have been passed down by the spoken word, as folklore. The stories are part myth and part real. The following are some of the most famous.

Los Amantes de Teruel (The Lovers of Teruel)

In the early years of the thirteenth century, there lived in the town of Teruel, near Valencia, a young man, Diego Martínez de Marcilla, and a young girl, Isabel de Segura. Both were from good families. The two had been friends since childhood. As adults, they fell in love. Diego asked Isabel's father, Don Pedro de Segura, for her hand in marriage. Don Pedro, however, knew that Diego had an older brother who would inherit his father's wealth. So he rejected Diego's request. Diego pleaded with Don Pedro to give him five years to obtain enough wealth to allow him to marry Isabel. Don Pedro agreed, thinking that he would find a more suitable husband for his daughter while Diego was away. Diego went off to war to seek his fortune.

During the five years Diego was away, Isabel rejected the offers of other men to marry her. At the end of the five years, however, she had to marry. She agreed to marry a man, Señor Azagra, from the nearby village of Albarracín.

Shortly after the wedding took place, in the year 1217, Diego returned to Teruel. He brought with him the fortunes and riches of war that he had won. Once he found out that Isabel had married someone else, he went to her. He pleaded with her to give him one last kiss. Isabel refused, because she was now married. Heartbroken, Diego fell dead at the feet of his beloved.

Isabel's husband, Señor Azagra, arrived to find the dead body of Diego. He carried the body to the home of Diego's father, Don Martín de Marcilla. He left the body outside the door of Don Martín's house. Don Martín found the body of his son in the morning. He took him to be buried at the Church of San Pedro. During the funeral ceremony, a young woman, whose face was covered by a veil, approached the body. It was Isabel. She kneeled down. She lifted the veil from her face. She kissed the cold lips of her beloved Diego, a kiss she had refused him in the last moment of his life. At that moment, Isabel, too, fell dead by the side of Diego. Both died of broken hearts. They were buried together, side by side, in the same Church of San Pedro. Today the sculpted marble figures of the lovers of Teruel, Isabel and Diego, lie on the cover of their tombs. Both have an arm extended toward each other between the tombs, their hands touching for eternity.

El Cid

The background to the legend of El Cid is the Reconquest (La Reconquista). The time was between the years 1050 and 1100. Christians were fighting against the Muslim invaders who had occupied Spain for 350 years, since 711. Sometimes they fought alone, as Christians. Sometimes they fought with Muslims whose enemies were the same as theirs. It was a time of changing loyalties by both Christians and Muslims.

The man who became known as El Cid (from the Arabic *sidi,* meaning "lord") was Rodrigo (also called Ruy) Díaz de Vivar. He was born in Vivar, near Burgos in Castile, in about 1043. He was brought up in the court of King Ferdinand I of Castile. When Ferdinand died in 1065, his eldest son, Sancho, became King Sancho II of Castile. Sancho appointed Rodrigo to be commander of his royal troops. In 1067, Rodrigo and Sancho brought the Muslim king of Zaragoza in northeast Spain, al-Muqtadir, under the control of Castile.

Ferdinand I left another of his kingdoms, León, to his second son, Alfonso VI. Sancho waged war on Alfonso, with the help of Rodrigo, to take León for himself. The legend of El Cid says that Rodrigo did not want to support Sancho against his brother Alfonso. In fact, Rodrigo played a large part in Sancho's successful campaigns against Alfonso. Sancho was killed in 1072 without leaving an heir to his throne. Alfonso became king once again. Rodrigo had fought against Alfonso, but Alfonso allowed Rodrigo to remain in his court.

A fourteenth-century illumination from the *Chronicles of Spain* in which El Cid is portrayed as a loyal soldier who helped liberate Spain from the Moors. El Cid continues to represent the Spanish ideal of patriotic heroism.

Rodrigo married King Alfonso's niece, Jimena. She was the daughter of the Count of Oviedo, in León. By marrying Jimena, Rodrigo became linked with the royal dynasty of León. They had two daughters and one son.

In 1081, Rodrigo led a raid against the Muslim kingdom of Toledo, which was under Alfonso's protection. Alfonso punished Rodrigo for that, sending him into exile. Rodrigo offered his services to the Muslim ruler of Zaragoza, al-Mu'tamin. In the service of al-Mu'tamin and his successor, al-Musta'in II, Rodrigo fought against Christian forces for nearly ten years. In 1094, the Muslim ruler of Valencia, Ibn Jahhaf, surrendered the city to Rodrigo after a long siege. Although Rodrigo officially held Valencia on behalf of Alfonso VI, he actually ruled the city as his own.

Rodrigo died in Valencia in July 1099. His body was taken back to Castile. It was buried in the monastery of San Pedro de Cardeña, near Burgos. The legend of El Cid grew from that time on. El Cid became a hero of all Spain, even though he fought for both Christians and Muslims during his lifetime. The greatest monument to his legend is the epic poem *El Cantar de Mío Cid* (The Song of the Cid), sometimes known as *El Poema de Mío Cid* (The poem of the Cid). The poem was written by an unknown author around 1140. Rodrigo was a legend in his own lifetime. After his death, he became a legend for all time as El Cid, the greatest heroic figure in the history of Spain.

La Chanson de Roland

La Chanson de Roland is an epic poem inspired by the struggle between Muslims and Christians in Spain. It was written in old French around 1100. The poem was based on the Battle of Roncesvalles in the year 778. Emperor Charlemagne had been fighting the Muslims in Spain. He was taking his army back to France through the Pass of Roncesvalles, high up in the Pyrenees north of Pamplona. A band of local Basque fighters attacked the rear guard of his army. The Basques massacred the French soldiers before the rest of the army could get back to help. Roland was one of the rear guard commanders killed in the attack.

The battle with the Basques was actually a minor skirmish. It became a legend, however, because of the tragic-heroic figure of Roland. The background is the struggle between the Muslims and Christians. In *La Chanson de Roland*, Roland is Charlemagne's nephew. He is accompanied by a trusted friend, Oliver. Ganelon is one of the commanders of Charlemagne's army. Ganelon tells the Muslim king of Zaragoza, Marsile, the position of the retreating Christian army. Marsile takes a force of 400,000 men and attacks the 20,000 rear guard troops of the army at Roncesvalles. Roland is too proud to blow his ivory horn to call the rest of the army back to help. Finally he does blow his horn. The rest of the army returns. But they find Roland and all the rear guard troops dead.

The Battle of Roncesvalles became the legend of Roland: the chivalrous, loyal, and courageous knight who, tragically but heroically, sacrifices himself for his Christian king fighting against the non-Christian enemy. Oliver is the wise and trusted loyal friend. Ganelon is the traitor. Roland the tragic hero was the inspiration for many later French and Italian epic poems. The historical background to all these works was the struggle between Christians and Muslims in Spain and a massacre in the Pass of Roncesvalles in 778 where a proud *paladin* (knight), Roland, died for his Christian king.

In the Battle of Roncesvalles *(right)*, Roland and his army were defeated by the Moors because of the betrayal of a "loyal" companion, Ganelon; an ambush by the Moors; and the small number of French troops. Charlemagne, returning to witness the bloody battlefield, honored Roland for his bravery.

Shown here is a 1648 map of Santiago de Compostela, an important Christian site of pilgrimage. Christians traveled to the grave of Saint James as early as the tenth century. After the Moors invaded Spain, the image of Saint James evolved from a gentle martyr to a fierce Christian warrior. Today, Saint James is Spain's patron saint.

Santiago de Compostela

There are many different versions of the legend of Santiago. Santiago is Spanish for St. James. (Santiago is a version of San Diego, or St. James.) Details of the legend have been added to and changed over many centuries. The basic legend, however, is as follows.

After the death of Jesus Christ, one of his apostles, James the Elder, traveled around the Iberian Peninsula to convert the people to Christianity. He returned to Judea in AD 44. The ruler of Judea, Herod Agrippa, had him tortured and put to death for preaching the gospel of Christ. James's death made him a martyr (a person who dies for his religious beliefs). Herod forbade the other disciples from burying the body of James. They stole the body during the night. They placed it on a marble slab on board a small boat. They pushed the boat out to sea. It drifted to the coast of Galicia, in northwest Spain. There, the body of James on the marble slab was found and buried at a secret place in a wood. Many centuries later, in the year 813 (some say 840), there was a hermit, Pelayo, who lived in the woods. One night he saw a bright light and heard music that led him to where James was buried, near a village called Padrón. A local bishop, Teodomiro, announced that the bones found at the site were those of St. James—Santiago. A shrine was built there.

The shrine became a holy place of pilgrimage. The city that developed around the shrine became Santiago de Compostela. This name is from the Latin, *Campus Stellae* (Compostella), "field of stars," meaning the bright lights that led the hermit Pelayo to the site. The Camino de Santiago (the road to Santiago) is the route across northern

An illustration from *Le Chanson de Roland*. Roland blew his horn at the Battle of Roncesvalles so loudly that the earth shook and birds fell from the trees. Roland and the troops of Charlemagne's army were massacred at Roncesvalles. Even today, Basque mountaineers say that on stormy nights in the Pyrenees they hear the echo of the horn.

Spain that pilgrims follow to get to the shrine of Santiago. Today, thousands of people travel the Camino de Santiago as modern pilgrims. It is one of the most important pilgrimages for Christians to experience.

The symbol of Santiago is a scallop shell. Some people say the reason for this is because a knight on a horse plunged into the sea when the horse was frightened by seeing the boat with James's body drifting toward the coast. The knight, according to the legend, saved himself by climbing on board the boat. His clothes were covered in scallop shells. Pilgrims to the shrine therefore carried scallop shells during their pilgrimage. They used the shells for eating and drinking. Pilgrims to Santiago believe that angels guided the boat carrying James's body to Galicia. They follow the route to Santiago to show their belief in divine guidance, whereby God forgives them their sins.

SPANISH FESTIVALS AND CEREMONIES OF ANTIQUITY AND TODAY

5

Every day is fiesta day in Spain. This is because all the regions, as well as the 8,000 small towns and villages in Spain, each have a special day of the year they celebrate as their own. Some of these fiestas last a day, some a few days, some as long as a month (in larger, richer towns). Many people who have left their town or village for the big city return to their hometown every year to participate in the local fiesta. In the past the celebrations were often religious. In modern Spain, however, they have become more secular, civic events (but often preceded by some

religious ceremony). Usually they are celebrated in the name the patron saint of the village, town, city, or region. The patron saint of all of Spain, for example, is St. James (Santiago, in Spanish).

There is at least one saint to commemorate for every day of the year. Most people in Spain are Roman Catholic. Their first names are commonly names of saints. They celebrate their saint's day (which is called their *onomástica*, in Spanish) much more than their birthday (*cumpleaño*).

Saints days were celebrated with great feasts in the early days of the Catholic Church. This is why saints days are also called feast days. The words "fiesta" and "festival" come from *festa*, the Latin word for "feast."

Human-pyramid building *(left)*, a serious sport in Spain, is practiced at town festivals like this one at Tarragona. For hundreds of years, castellers, human-pyramid builders in the Spanish region of Catalonia, have used their bodies to form skyscrapers as high as five-story buildings. Decorative lights are hung throughout the streets in Jerez *(above)* in preparation for Christmas. Christmas season in Spain starts on December 8 with the Feast of the Immaculate Conception and a dance performed by children in front of Seville's cathedral. In Spain, the three wise men bring gifts on Epiphany, January 6.

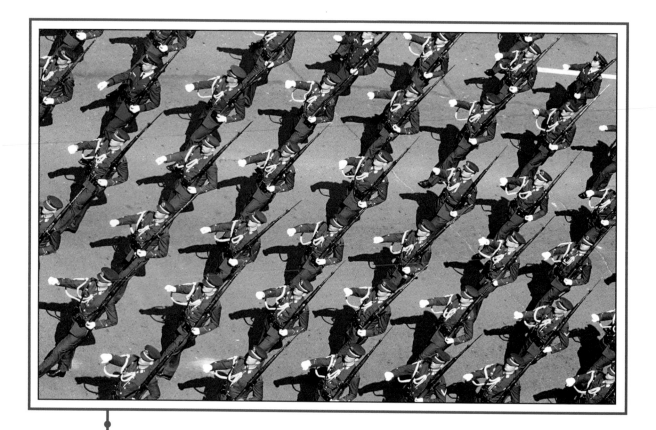

A military parade on Spain's National Day, October 12. On that day in 1492, Christopher Columbus first set foot in the New World. He was soon followed by the conquistadors who imposed Spanish culture throughout Central and South America. National Day was created by the Spanish government in 1977 to celebrate the heritage of Spanish culture. This national holiday is also known as Dia del Hispanica.

There are also national holidays. They include New Year's Day, Good Friday, and Easter (including Easter Monday in most places). Labor Day, on May 1, is called May Day in other countries. On Assumption Day, or Feast of the Assumption, on August 15, people celebrate the day the Virgin Mary ascended to heaven. Spanish National Day, on October 12, is the day Columbus made his first landfall in the New World. All Saints Day on November 1, known as All Souls' Day in English, commemorates dead ancestors. December 6 is Constitution Day, the time to celebrate the Spanish Constitution. Christmas is on December 25. Many of the days are religions occasions as Spain actively celebrates being a Roman Catholic country.

Other festivals in Spain include the celebration of the wine harvest at the end of September and early October, and the blessing of animals on St. Anthony's Day, January 17. During Moors and Christians Day, held at Alcoy (near Valencia), people reenact a battle every year in memory of a famous victory by the Christians over the Moors

People race through the streets of Pamplona for the running of the bulls during the week-long festival of San Fermín. Each morning for a week, six bulls run to the stadium where they will fight and die. People participating in the event carry rolled up newspapers to swat the bulls.

(Muslims) in 1276, which was supposedly led by St. George (Alcoy's patron saint). The National Cheese Festival, at Trujillo, in the west of Spain, is in April and May. A classical theater festival takes place in the old Roman amphitheater of Mérida, in the west of Spain, during July and August. A guitar festival in Coroba, in southern Spain, is held in July, and the International Jazz Festivals of San Sebastián and Vitoria are held in northern Spain, in July. The International Film Festival at San Sebastián is in September.

One of the most spectacular festivals in Spain is Las Fallas, held in Valencia in March. On St. Joseph's Day (March 19), in the Middle Ages, the guilds (societies) of carpenters of Valencia burned the wooden

Children dress up for the Fiesta de Moros y Cristianos in Spain. Celebrated in many coastal towns, this festival is most spectacular in Alcoy. One weekend every April, citizens of Alcoy erect a large papier-mâché castle in the town plaza and reenact the Battle of Alcoy, which was fought between the Christians and the Moors in 1276.

Too Many Tomatoes?

You may want to make a special trip to Spain for the festival of the tomato. Huge cartloads of ripe tomatoes are driven into the main square of the town of Buñol, in Valencia. Then there is a battle of tomatoes as thousands of people throw tons of tomatoes at each other! The festival is held on the last Wednesday of August.

candleholders they used in winter to light their workshops. This ceremony celebrated the coming of spring. Nowadays, huge wooden and papier-mâché statues are paraded through the streets. When the processions have finished, the statues are burned in the streets. There is also a spectacular fireworks display.

Many places in Spain have local festivals or pilgrimages to honor the Virgin Mary. The most famous is the Rocío, or Our Lady of the Dew (*Rocío* means "dew" in Spanish), at Almonte, near Huelva in the southwest. As many as a million people gather for Rocío. The Virgen del Pilar (Our Lady of the Pillar), at Zaragoza, in northeast Spain, is a spectacular festival because of the large number of flowers in the procession.

Holy Week (Semana Santa)

The biggest festival of the year for most Spaniards is the week leading up to Easter, known as Holy Week (Semana Santa).

Pilgrims walk in the procession of Our Lady of the Dew, held during the weekend of Pentecost. One million people journey on horseback or in horse-drawn wagons to gather at the shrine. Dating from the fifteenth century, this festival draws believers who claim the statue of the Virgin has the power to cure disease, infertility, and mental disorders.

Processions are held in villages, towns, and cities throughout Spain. The weeklong Feria de Abril (April Fair) at Seville comes two weeks after Holy Week. It is one of the most beautiful and popular festivals in Spain. The festivities last through the night. Every day there are processions of riders on horseback who are dressed in traditional Andalusian costumes.

During Holy Week, up to fifty men carry an image of the Virgin Mary through the streets of Castilleja de la Cuesta. Floats called *pasos* are decorated with statues related to the crucifixion of Jesus. The wooden statues are painted to look like waxwork. The floats are accompanied by a bugle or tuba band and 1,000 robed "Nazarenes."

Holy Week processions, held from Good Friday to Easter Sunday, date back to the Middle Ages. Statues of the Virgin Mary and of Christ are carried through the streets on heavy wooden platforms. A dozen or more men stand hidden under the platforms, carrying them on their shoulders. Brass bands and drummers play religious music to accompany them through the streets. In some of the bigger cities, such as Seville and Madrid, hooded, robed men carry the statues. These are members of so-called cofraternities, or brotherhoods (*hermandades*), of the Catholic Church.

Individuals often walk along with the processions. These people might walk barefoot or have chains attached to their ankles so that they suffer some pain. They are penitents, or people who are suffering pain or sorrow for their sins. They are

Julián López Escobar, or El Juli, is the youngest bullfighter in the history of bull-fighting. At age nine, he entered Madrid's prestigious Escuela Taurina, a school for bullfighting. His instructors immediately recognized his natural talent. Having won worldwide respect, he is carried from the bullring on the shoulders of adoring fans.

imitating the pain and suffering of Christ's walk to the Hill of Calvary where he was crucified. By suffering in this way (and through prayer), they believe that their sins are forgiven.

Bullfighting

The most famous fiesta of Spain is bullfighting, known as the *fiesta nacional* (national festival). It is celebrated more in some parts of Spain than in others. Its most enthusiastic aficionados (fans, or followers) are in the south and central parts of Spain. It is least popular among Catalans in the northeast region of Catalonia. The single most famous bullfighting fiesta of Spain is the running of the bulls during the annual San Fermín Festival in Pamplona in July.

Bullfighting is a ritualistic spectacle, a festival. It is not a sport between two equals. The bull never wins! (Newspapers in Spain publish their reports on bullfights in the culture section, not the sports section.) The fiesta nacional refers to the *corrida de toros* (bullfight) in general, but there are many different forms of corrida (some of which are not actually called corridas). Some bullfights use young bulls (calves) of different ages. Some are fought only from horseback. Some do not have picadors (men on horseback who weaken the bull with sharp lances).

Most bullfights in Spain coincide with a town's local patron saint fiesta or festival. Therefore, these take place just once a year. Small towns cannot afford to hold regular bullfights, so the corrida becomes the central part of their annual festival. For the bigger cities, like Madrid, Valencia, Seville, and Barcelona, there is a *temporada* (season) of bull-fights that takes place usually on Sundays afternoons, from March or April until October.

All the men who fight the bull in a corrida are *toreros* (bullfighters). (There have only ever been a few successful women bullfighters.) The team of toreros in a corrida is the *cuadrilla*. The matador (which literally means "killer") is the main torero of the

Nowadays the bullfight is controversial. Many Spaniards believe it should no longer be a part of their modern European culture. Others believe it is the one symbol of Spain that makes the country different. Many non-Spaniards think it is a cruel spectacle that should be abolished.

cuadrilla. He is the one who kills the bull. Other members of the cuadrilla are *picadores* (picadors), who ride on horseback with a long lance that they stick in the bull's neck to wound and weaken it. Banderilleros run toward the bull and stick two sharp pointed darts (banderillas) in its neck to weaken it even more. And peones (or *mozos*), are assistants in the ring. Some matadors are famous throughout Spain and even in Latin America, where many of them fight in the winter months. The best bullfighters are millionaires.

The standard format of a bullfight is strictly regulated. Three matadors have two bulls to kill each, alternately. The matador has twenty minutes to play and eventually kill the bull. The twenty minutes are divided into three parts (*tercios*): first go the picadors, then the banderilleros, and finally the matador, who kills the bull. The peones stand around the barrier of the bullring to help out when the matador and the other toreros need them.

The matador kills by stepping in toward the bull and reaching over the bull's head (and horns) with his sword (*estoque*). He aims the estoque between the bull's shoulder blades. The estoque is supposed to sever the bull's aorta (main artery) when it goes in. He tries to keep the bull's head down (so it does not raise its head, and horns, into his body) by holding a small cape (muleta) in his other hand, waving it under the bull's nose. If the matador severs the aorta with a clean kill, the bull dies instantly. If not, he tries again, and if necessary, a few more times. If he does not get the sword in after two or three attempts, he kills the bull with a small dagger thrust into the bull's neck. This severs the bull's spinal cord and kills it. When the bull is dead, it is dragged out of the ring by a team of horses. At a place just outside the ring, the bull's carcass is butchered. The meat is sold to the public.

THE RELIGIONS OF SPAIN THROUGHOUT ITS HISTORY

6

U ntil 1978, Roman Catholicism was the official religion of Spain (*nacional-catolicismo*, national Catholicism). The 1978 Constitution changed that. It separated the church from the state. It guaranteed the right of every citizen to practice any religion. It still allowed for a degree of discrimination in favor of Catholicism, but it pointed toward future reforms (such as divorce and abortion) that the Catholic Church opposed.

Catholicism in Spain has roots that go back to Roman and Visigothic times. The Romans introduced Christianity into Spain in the second century AD. Roman power collapsed during the fifth century when Germanic tribes (Suebians, Alans, Vandals, and finally Visigoths) invaded the peninsula. After the Visigoths invaded Rome in the year 410, the Roman Empire quickly declined.

In AD 589, the Visigoth king Recared recognized that most people living in the Iberian Peninsula (Spain was not a country yet) were Catholics. He therefore converted to Catholicism. Other Visigoth nobles and bishops soon followed. The Hispano-Romans in Spain at that time were already Catholic. The Visigoth king Swinthila, who ruled from 621 to 631, defeated the last non-Catholic

A stone relief dating from around 1520 depicts the compulsory baptism of Moorish women at the conquest of Granada *(left)*. Cardinal Ximenes, an inquisitor on behalf of the Catholic Monarchs, ordered the expulsion from Spain of Moors who refused to be baptized. Baptisms were given en mass and so quickly that there was no time for religious instruction for the new converts. An estimated 50,000 to 70,000 Moors were forcibly baptized in this way at Granada. Saint Ignatius *(above)* traveled to Rome and the Holy Land to convert Muslims to Christianity. His mediations and insights led to the formation of the Jesuits in 1534.

The Mezquita, or Great Mosque of Córdoba, was built in 786 by Emir Abd-ar Rahman. In 964, the mihrab (inner sanctuary) was topped with a mosaic-covered dome. Capturing Córdoba in 1236, Ferdinand III built a Christian church within the walls of the mosque, converting the minaret, the tall spire structure, into a belfry.

inhabitants in Spain, the Byzantines. From then on, the whole peninsula was united under Catholic Visigoth authority.

The Moors (Muslims from North Africa) introduced Islam into Spain when they invaded in 711. Islam became the dominant religion in southern Spain, and the Christians were driven into northern Spain. Over the next 800 years, the Christians fought to regain the territory occupied by the Muslim invaders. This period of Christians fighting against Muslims is known as La Reconquista (the Reconquest). The religion of Islam did not last in Spain after the Moors were expelled in 1492. The Islamic culture, however, had a huge influence on Spanish art, architecture, science, literature (especially poetry), and even on the Spanish language (Castilian). Many of Spain's architectural treasures are fine examples of Islamic art. The Muslims of Al-Andalus (Andalusia) who made the pilgrimage to Mecca brought back the fruits of their learning from Arab culture. Mathematics and science, for example, were much more advanced in the Arabic Islamic civilization than they were in the European Christian civilization at that time.

When the Moors first invaded Spain in 711, the population of the Iberian Peninsula was 4 to 5 million. Within a hundred years, Muslims from Islamic countries comprised about 10 percent of that population. There was also quite a large number of ex-Christians who converted to Islam. The Jewish population was around 150,000 to 200,000. Overall, Christians were the great majority on the peninsula throughout the Islamic period, even in southern Spain where Islam dominated. The number of Christians increased in the 1300s and 1400s. That was because the Jews

in Spain had become persecuted. Many of them converted to Christianity. They were known as *los conversos* (the converted).

The Reyes Católicos (the Catholic Monarchs, Ferdinand and Isabella) strengthened the dominant position of Catholicism in Spain. In 1492, they expelled the last Muslims, and then all the Jews, from Spain. There was a lot of hostility toward Spanish Jews (including los conversos) at this time. Christians were jealous of them because many had become wealthy.

The Reyes Católicos took advantage of that hostility. They established the Inquisition in 1478, with the consent of Pope Sixtus IV in Rome. The Inquisition was a kind of brutal police force used to get rid of the Jews and all other non-Catholics in Spain. It used informers, torture, terror, and secrecy to find and expose heretics (people whose beliefs were

A thirteenth-century illustration from *The Songs of Saint Mary* depicts the Turks and Moors regaining their castle. Alfonso X, called Alfonso the Wise, who ruled Castile and Léon from 1252 to 1284, commissioned this work. While politically unsuccessful, Alfonso X promoted education throughout his country. He implemented a code of laws for his people and made Castilian Spain's official language. To promote learning, Alfonso X commissioned the writing of Spain's history and the creation of an encyclopedia.

The illustration here depicts a procession of victims during an *auto-da-fé*, or act of faith. Beginning in 1481, people accused of lapsing in the practice of Christianity were burned at the stake. Over the next twelve years, thousands of "heretics" were tried and burned. Dressed in penitent's gowns, the accused marched to the stake and were urged to repent. Those who confessed were strangled before the fire was lit. People who refused to repent were burned alive. Lasting 327 years, the Spanish Inquisition was finally abolished in 1808.

different from the conventional beliefs of Catholicism). The Inquisition was, in effect, a reign of terror. Today we would call it ethnic cleansing. Its aims were, first, to get rid of heretics and their "evil influence" on society; second, to strengthen the power of the monarchy (Ferdinand and Isabella); and third, to establish Catholicism once and for all as the only acceptable religion in Spain.

The first inquisitor general of the Inquisition was Tomás de Torquemada. (He was actually from a converso family himself.) In 1492, Torquemada persuaded Ferdinand and Isabella to expel from Spain all the Jews who refused to be baptized as Christians. Ferdinand and Isabella expelled from Spain around 170,000 Jews. They were known as the Sephardic Jews, or Sephardi (from the Hebrew for "Spain," *Sefarad*). Today there are around 750,000 Sephardi. Most live in Israel, but there are Sephardi in many other countries, as well.

Most of the 300,000 or so conversos remained in Spain as Orthodox Catholics. Quite a few conversos played a large role in Spain's great Siglo de Oro (Golden Century) of cultural achievements in the sixteenth and seventeenth centuries. Jews and conversos in Spain had become a dominant group among the small educated elite of fourteenth- and fifteenth-century Spain. The conversos rejected their Talmudic heritage. They looked for new stimulation in the Christian world of the Renaissance that surrounded them. Hostility toward them by traditional Christians might have spurred them on to excel in their newly adopted Christian culture. This is one possible explanation why so many ex-Jewish Christian conversos went on to become such great figures of Spanish civilization between the sixteenth and eighteenth centuries. The Jewish religion as such became insignificant in Spain after 1492. Its cultural influences, however, were hugely significant for the next 300 years.

Religion in Twentieth-Century Spain

The Catholic religion in Spain in the twentieth century was, for most of the time, closely related to the state. The Catholic Church supported Franco and his dictatorship as a symbol of nationalism and patriotism. It was closely tied to extreme right-wing politics, as well as to the land-owning elite. It restricted the evolution of a more liberal, free thinking society in Spain in general. This created conflicts. Some Spaniards had ideas and values that were strictly guided by Catholic principles and doctrine. Others were Catholic by religious conviction, but had their own ideas and ethics that were different from Catholic dogma. Others were officially Catholic, but were, in private, opposed to the Church as an institution.

During the Spanish Civil War, the Catholic Church chose to be on the side of the nationalists. They opposed the "godless

General Franco's mausoleum is located in Valle de los Caídos (Valley of the Fallen). Beneath a huge cross is a granite chapel that is only slightly smaller than the one at the Vatican. Republican prisoners of war were forced to excavate the rock for this monument after the Spanish Civil War.

A nineteenth-century engraving of Ferdinand VII swearing in the constitution. Napoléon invaded Spain in 1808, capturing King Ferdinand VII. The Spanish fought to save their country. When Ferdinand VII was restored to the throne in 1814, he abolished the constitution of 1812. Revolutionaries who had once fought for him staged an uprising. In 1820, Ferdinand VII reinstated the constitution.

Communism" of the Republicans. After the war, Franco rewarded the Church by giving it great authority over secular (nonreligious) matters.

The Church had great power over the public education system in particular. The legal system was based on Catholic morality that prohibited, for example, divorce and abortion. (Divorce has been allowed only since 1981, and abortion [in limited circumstances] since 1985.) All marriages had to be in church if either the bride or groom were baptized (that is, Catholic). The Church exercised control over many aspects of intellectual, moral, and cultural life. A strict Catholic morality was the basis for all kinds of censorship: in the movies, literature, popular media such as magazines, and even in personal activities. Dancing in public by people under the age of eighteen, for example, was forbidden. So was kissing in public. Such "offenses" of "blasphemy" and "public scandal" were only removed from the penal code in 1987. By that time, however, they were, in practice, virtually ignored.

Under Franco's dictatorship (1939–1975), no political parties were allowed except for the Falange party. (The official name for the Falange party was Falange Española Tradicionalista y de las Juntas de Ofensiva Nacional-Sindicalista, or Traditional Spanish Phalanx of the Factions of the National Trades Union Offensive). For most of Franco's regime, dictatorial power and the Catholic Church went hand in hand.

World War II ended with the defeat of Fascist regimes in Germany and Italy. Spain was neutral in World War II. Right after the war, there was a lot of support worldwide for left-wing (Socialist, Communist) opposition to right-wing Fascist forces. This was especially so among the proletarian (working) classes. Socialism and other left-wing movements were based on the principle of proletarian ideals. In many cases this included atheism.

The Roman Catholic Church was losing a lot of support to the left-wing movements. The Church planned a worldwide program to help bring back support, especially in the workplace, by setting up Catholic workers' organizations. In Spain there were two kinds of organizations: Hermandades Obreras de Acción Católica, or HOAC (Workers Brotherhoods for Catholic Action), and Juventud Obrera Católica, or JOC (Catholic Workers Youth Organizations). The aim of HOAC and JOC was to defend Catholic principles of social justice. That, ultimately, brought them into conflict with Franco's regime. State Fascism's control of the people depended on dictatorial power, not social justice.

The 1962–1965 Second Vatican Council (a gathering of Catholic bishops worldwide) raised questions about how repressive regimes, even if they were Catholic (like Franco's), could be compatible with Christian values. As a result, the Catholic Church in Spain began to distance itself from the Franco dictatorship. Franco suppressed the Church's opposition. He even established a special jail for priests!

After Franco's death, the Church in Spain leaned increasingly toward democracy. A major figure in this movement was Cardinal Vicente Enrique y Tarancón (1907–1994). Cardinal Tarancón defended traditional Catholic policies, but called for greater democracy in religious life. That included the acceptance of religious pluralism (allowing other faiths to exist alongside Catholicism) and the separation of church and state.

By the 1980s, Spain was becoming an increasingly secular society. Almost all Spaniards were still Catholic, but only 25 to 30 percent of them actually attended church regularly. There was also a decline in the number of priests. In 1961, 825 men were ordained as priests. In 1981, just 163 were ordained. Throughout the 1980s, many priests applied to leave the priesthood (mainly because of the celibacy law). By the 1990s, there was a shortage of priests. The Church could not provide a priest for every parish. There were only 20,000 priests for 22,000 parishes.

Catholicism is still by far the dominant religion in Spain. Almost all Spaniards are Catholic (at least officially). There is a big difference, however, between the role of religion in Spain now and its importance in the past when Spaniards were more or less forced to be Catholic. Most are still Catholic now. The difference is that today they have the democratic right and individual freedom to choose other options.

THE ART AND ARCHITECTURE OF SPAIN

7

A s you walk around the centers of towns and cities in Spain, you are surrounded by old, big, and ornate buildings. Many of these buildings were constructed hundreds of years ago. They often have balconies with wrought ironwork outside the windows. This is the typical heavy style of Spanish architecture. It dates from a time when builders used craftsmen to carve stone into elaborate shapes to adorn the fronts of their buildings. Inside public buildings you might see even more elaborate decorations on columns, walls, ceilings, and windows. But it is the facades of the older buildings, with their heavy, ornate style, that characterize Spain's urban architecture.

Around the outsides of towns and cities, the style is mainly from the 1950s and 1960s. There was a massive migration of people away from the countryside in Spain at that time, toward the cities. New housing was built as the population of cities grew. The architecture of these modern suburban areas is characterized by apartment buildings, usually four or five stories high. Some have window balconies and other features in the Mediterranean style. Otherwise, and more usually, they are very plain, especially in contrast with the old baroque buildings in the town and city centers. In the 1980s and 1990s, Spanish architects began to build more imaginatively. Nowadays there

The Temple of the Sagrada Familia in Barcelona *(left)* is an unfinished masterpiece by the great Catalan architect Antoni Gaudí. Honoring the Holy Family, the cathedral combines modern elements with gothic style. Twelve spires represent the apostles, although only eight are complete. Begun in 1882, construction continues to this day. *Las Meninas* (The Maids of Honor) *(above)*, painted by Diego Rodriguez Velázquez, was commissioned by Philip IV as a portrait of his daughter. It was completed in 1656 as Philip IV struggled to protect Spain from Protestant Europe. Shadowy figures in the background may represent a nun and monk, through which Velázquez shows the constant presence of the Church.

are many more stylish buildings. These include suburban apartment buildings with a contemporary Mediterranean style. Glass and steel office buildings in the modern style are everywhere. The genuinely Spanish architecture, however, is fortunately still found within the heart of cities and towns all around Spain.

Spain's Artistic Heritage

Art in Spain was first created many thousands of years before Spain became a country. The earliest prehistoric inhabitants, Celtic people from the north and from the rest of Europe (Phoenecians, Goths, Greeks, Romans), the Moorish invaders from Islamic North Africa, and influences from other European art movements (the Renaissance, for example) have all contributed to the richness of Spain's artistic heritage. Today that heritage is highly visible in the varied architectural styles of its buildings and in the wealth of art treasures in the country's public museums, commercial galleries, and private collections.

The earliest representations of art in Spain are prehistoric cave paintings from 15,000 to 20,000 years ago. The most famous are from the Cuevas de Altamira in

Cantabria on the north coast, about twenty miles west of Santander. A local hunter first discovered the paintings in these caves in 1868. Later, in 1875, a nobleman from Santander, Marcelino de Sautuola, visited the site but found just bones and old flint tools. A few years later he returned with his daughter. She noticed paintings of bison on the walls of the caves. Sautuola published descriptions of the paintings, but art experts rejected them as forgeries. The paintings were only accepted later, in the early

The Lady of Elche, a stone Iberian statue, dates from the fifth century BC. A woman with an elaborate headdress, she may portray a goddess or Iberian princess. On the back of the statue is a small hole, possibly for the deposit of ashes of the deceased.

1900s, as genuine prehistoric art. The caves are now closed to the general public. They were in danger of being ruined by human contact.

The Iberian tribes were early inhabitants of the Iberian Peninsula. Very little of their culture remains today. The most famous surviving Iberian artwork is a small stone statue known as La Dama de Elche (The Lady of Elche). The statue was found in Alcudia, near the town of Elche in the Alicante province, on August 4, 1897. It dates from the fifth century BC. It was bought by a French archaeologist and exhibited in the Louvre museum in Paris. In 1941, it was returned to Spain. It is now at the National Archaeology Museum in Madrid. La Dama de Elche has been written about and studied numerous times. Still, it is not known whether she represents an Iberian goddess or an Iberian female beauty, or if she was created for some other purpose. She is, for that reason, a symbol of mystery and fascination.

There are, by contrast with the Iberians, many visible remains of the Roman occupation of Spain. Most of these are architectural, such as remains of Roman walls in cities including Barcelona and, just to the south, Tarragona. The Romans also built aqueducts, public baths, paved streets, sewers, amphitheaters, and, of course, houses to live in. These types of Roman architecture can still be seen in Spain. One of the most famous and impressive reminders

El Puente, located in Segovia, is a Roman aqueduct built in the first century AD under the rule of Emperor Trajan. The granite aqueduct, which stretches 10 miles (16 km) from the Frío River to the city of Segovia, is 93.5 feet (28.4 meters) high.

The Alhambra overlooks the city of Granada. A masterpiece of Moorish architecture in southern Spain, the Alhambra's design includes slender columns, fountains, and light-reflecting pools of water. Inside the palace, the artwork depicts scenes of men and nature. It was originally built as a fortress containing a palace and a small city within its walls. In 1238, the Alhambra was expanded by the Moors, who ruled southern Spain for 800 years.

of Roman architecture is the aqueduct at Segovia. It was built by the emperor Trajan who reigned from AD 98–117. It remains in use to this day, carrying water from the River Frío to Segovia, ten miles away. Its most spectacular feature is its series of 165 arches, stacked in two levels.

Spain's Islamic period (711–1492) produced even more surviving structures than the Roman era. The great Alhambra palace in Granada is a masterpiece of Islamic architecture. It was built mainly between 1238 and 1358 by Ibn al-Ahmar and his successors, the Moorish kings of Granada at that time. The interior stucco walls are intricately engraved. The palace stands on a hill overlooking a complex of elaborate gardens known as the Generalife (from the Arabic *Jannat al-'Arif*, meaning "garden of the builder"). The Alhambra and Generalife are now UNESCO World Heritage sites.

Nearby, in the old Moorish city of Córdoba, stands the Mezquita de Córdoba (Great Mosque of Córdoba), another jewel in the architectural crown of Islamic

Spain. It was converted into a Christian cathedral in the thirteenth century. This is why it is also known as the Mosque-Cathedral of Cordoba. The original mosque was built by 'Abd ar-Rahman I from 784 to 786. It was enlarged over the following 200 years, making it one of Islam's largest sacred sites. Córdoba was taken over by King Ferdinand III of Castile in 1236. The mosque was converted to a Christian cathedral. A high altar and other Christian features (chapels, a belfry) were added later. The Mezquita stands as a supreme example of Islamic architecture overlain by Christian features, reflecting the combination of Islamic and Christian influences in Spain's cultural heritage.

There are many other examples of Islamic influences in Spanish architecture and art. The typical Islamic half-moon arch, for example, is copied in many non-Islamic structures. Houses in southern Spain, where Islamic influences were strongest, often still have inward-facing patios reminiscent of the Islamic style. In the sixteenth century, a lot of architecture in Spain was in the "plateresque" style (from the Spanish *platero*, meaning "silversmith"). This was characterized by intricate ornamental work like that created by silversmiths. It was influenced by the highly decorative Islamic style of earlier centuries.

From the sixteenth century onward, with the unification of Spain, architecture evolved in the more typically Spanish ornate and decorative style. A new wave of contemporary architecture has emerged since the end of the Franco dictatorship (1975). One of the most recent and most famous buildings is the newly built Guggenheim Museum in Bilbao. The original and dynamic design of this museum by American architect Frank Gehry has already attracted millions of visitors. Barcelona, Valencia, and Madrid, in particular, also have important new building projects admired for their originality by architects around the world.

The Great Spanish Artists

The first great Spanish artist was El Greco (1541–1614). His real name was Doménikos Theotokopoulos. He was called El Greco ("The Greek") while he lived in Italy, because he was actually born on the Greek island of Crete. At that time, Crete was part of the city state of Venice. El Greco went to study in Venice as a young man. He then went to Spain in 1577. He lived and worked for most of his life in Toledo, sixty miles southwest of Madrid. He painted mostly religious subjects that were commissioned by churches and monasteries in the city and surrounding areas. His masterpiece is a painting called *Entierro del Conde de Orgaz* (Burial of the Count of

Orgaz), completed in 1588. El Greco's paintings are distinctive for their brilliant clashing colors, their often mystical, supernatural qualities, and the distortion—particularly the elongation—of bodies. He died in Toledo in 1614.

Diego Velázquez (1599–1660) was one of the greatest painters in the world. Velázquez, unlike El Greco, painted everyday subjects of people doing everyday things. His early paintings in Seville were in the so-called *bodegones* style. These paintings depicted people in places where food and drink were served, such as taverns, inns, and cookhouses (bodegones). Velázquez became the royal painter at the court of King Philip IV in Madrid, where he spent most of his life. He painted portraits of the king and other nobility. His greatest masterpiece is *Las Meninas* (The Maids of Honor). Velázquez himself is in the painting. He is standing in front of a large canvas, with a paintbrush and palette in his hands. In 1659, a year before his death, he was made a knight of the Order of Santiago, Spain's highest honor.

Francisco de Zurbarán (1598–1664) lived almost exactly at the same time as Velázquez. An early painting, *Immaculate Conception*, is similar in its naturalistic style to Velázquez's. Zurbarán spent most of his life in Seville. He painted mostly religious subjects. This is possibly why he is not as well known as Velázquez who painted more

popular images. Another great Spanish painter of this time, also from Seville, was Bartolomé Esteban Murillo (1618–1682). Like Zurbarán, Murillo is famous for his religious paintings. And like both Zurbarán and Velázquez, Murillo learned the naturalistic style of painting in Seville. He later became Spain's most popular seventeenth-century religious painter in the more extravagant Baroque style.

Francisco de Goya (1746–1828) was another court painter,

Burial of the Count of Orgaz (left), reflecting a deep sense of Christianity, is one of El Greco's most popular works. The painting was commissioned by the Church of Santo Tomé in Toledo, where it still hangs, and it attracted an audience as soon as it was displayed. Francisco de Goya's sketch *Barbarians (above)* is part of his *Disasters of War* series, completed between 1808 and 1814. In this series, Goya reinforced the nineteenth-century realist movement of painting, portraying the atrocities of war.

first for Charles III and then his son, Charles IV. At the age of forty-seven, a serious illness left him completely deaf. Goya made a series of etchings, *Los desastres de la guerra* (The disasters of war), that are among his best-known works. They depict the horrific acts he witnessed during and just after the Spanish War of Independence when Napoléon occupied Spain (1808–1814). Goya left Spain in 1823. He settled in Bordeaux, France, where he died four years later. Goya's paintings, drawings, and etchings were realistic and often savage impressions of the troubled times in which he lived.

The most important twentieth-century Spanish artist was Pablo Picasso (1881–1973). He dominated the world of twentieth-century art. Born in Málaga, in southern Spain, Picasso studied art in Madrid and Barcelona. After his first trip to Paris in 1900, he lived

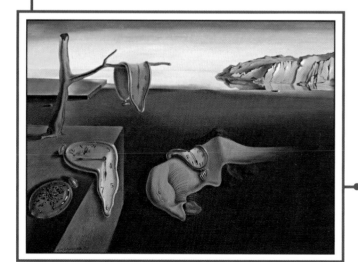

In *Guernica (above)*, painter Pablo Picasso expresses pain and anger caused by atrocities committed during the Spanish Civil War. Picasso was secretive about the piece and would not reveal hidden themes concealed in the overlapping imagery. *The Persistence of Memory (left)* is one of Salvador Dalí's most popular works. Dalí was one of the world's greatest surrealist painters. In *The Persistence of Memory*, time loses meaning. Dalí plays with the reality of hard objects by depicting drooping clocks.

The world famous Guggenheim Museum in Bilbao was completed in 1997. Designed by American architect Frank Gehry, the exterior of the building features interconnecting shapes. The museum occupies a 349,828-square-foot (32,500 sq m) site in Bilbao and has 118,403 square feet (11,000 sq m) of exhibition space, divided into nineteen galleries.

most of his life in France. After 1934, he never returned to Spain. Picasso's work includes thousands of paintings, drawings, etchings, sculptures, ceramics, and prints. He was best known as a founder of the cubist style of painting, but the range of his work and influence extended far beyond cubist. Velázquez, El Greco, Murillo, and Goya were the sources of his early inspiration. In 1937, he painted his masterpiece, *Guernica*. This huge painting is named for a Basque town, Gernika, bombed by the Germans in the Spanish Civil War. The images of this painting scream with the agony, horror, and tragedy of war. It is difficult to sum up the genius of Picasso because of the enormous variety of his artworks. No other artist of the twentieth century could equal Picasso's creative versatility, originality, and influence on the whole world of art.

Other important Spanish artists of the twentieth century were the Catalonian painter Joan (pronounced Zho-AN) Miró (1893–1983), the Catalonian surrealist artist Salvador Dalí (1904–1989), and Juan Gris (1887–1927), who, like Picasso, lived most of his life in France and was directly influenced by Picasso and cubism in Paris.

THE LITERATURE AND MUSIC OF SPAIN

8

T he first true Spanish work of literature was the poem about El Cid, *El Cantar de Mio Cid* (see chapter 4). The author of this epic poem is unknown. The original version was written in the mid-1200s. The only existing manuscript is from 1307. The last two of the three sections of the poem are an imaginary distortion of the historical facts about the heroic deeds of El Cid. It has survived in popularity to this today for its literary, rather than historical, qualities. Hollywood has made the story famous. The 1960s movie *El Cid* starred Charlton Heston and Sophia Loren.

There is a period in Spain's history called the Siglo de Oro (Golden Century, more often called the Golden Age in English, since it lasted more than a century). The Siglo de Oro for Spanish literature and art was the seventeenth century. Many of its greatest painters and three of its greatest writers all lived in the 1600s.

The greatest of all the writers was Miguel de Cervantes (1547–1616). He published his masterpiece, *Don Quixote*, at the beginning of the century. *Don Quixote* was the first great Spanish novel. It is still the greatest work of Spanish literature. Although Cervantes wrote many poems,

A nineteenth-century illustration of Don Quixote preparing his armor *(left)* appeared in a later edition of Miguel de Cervantes' novel *Don Quixote*. *Don Quixote* brought Cervantes immediate fame. After 1605, Cervantes' work was in demand because of the huge success of *Don Quixote*. A letter written to the archbishop of Toledo by Cervantes on March 26, 1616 *(above)*.

short stories, novels, and plays, none of them come close to the greatness of *Don Quixote*. Today that novel has been translated into dozens of languages. It has been read, studied, and analyzed by millions of students and critics. If only one work of literature could, on its own, represent all of Spanish literature, *Don Quixote* would be it.

Cervantes was born near Madrid in 1547. In 1569, he traveled to Italy and became a soldier. At the naval battle of Lepanto against the Turks, he was wounded and lost the use of his left hand. He and his brother Rodrigo sailed back to Spain in 1575. On the way they were captured by Barbary pirates off the coast of North Africa. Both were sold as slaves in Algiers. Rodrigo was freed after two years. Cervantes, because he was of greater rank and importance, had a higher ransom on his head. Finally, in 1580, his family was able to raise the 500 gold ducats ransom to set Cervantes free. He used these episodes and his life in Algiers later in his literary works.

A nineteenth-century portrait of Miguel de Cervantes. In *Don Quixote*, considered the first modern novel, Cervantes explored insights into the human mind and society's unwillingness to deviate from the norm. This was a revolutionary new approach to storytelling, which until 1605 had focused mainly on tales of romantic chivalry.

Back in Spain, Cervantes spent his time trying to make a living by writing poetry, plays, and stories. In 1587, he got a job supplying the Spanish navy with provisions. Over the next ten years, he was constantly looking for work, short of money, and spending time in jail for financial problems. It may have been while he was in the Crown Jail of Seville, from 1597 to 1598, that he had the idea of writing *Don Quixote*. In January 1605, Part I of Cervantes's masterpiece was published as *El ingenioso hidalgo Don Quixote de la Mancha* ("The ingenious nobleman Don Quixote of La Mancha," known simply as "Don Quixote"). It was an immediate success. Part II, *Segunda parte del ingenioso hidalgo Don Quixote de la Mancha*, came out in 1615. Parts I and II were first printed together as a single book in 1617.

At almost sixty years of age, Cervantes had written his first blockbuster. *Don Quixote*, the "knight of the woeful countenance," has come to symbolize, in the popular mind, the romantic idealist who sees the world through a veil of illusion. His companion Sancho Panza is the realist who sees the world as it is. *Don Quixote* was a pioneering work in the history of the novel. Its characters and plot immediately captured the imagination of the public. Future great novelists recognized in *Don Quixote* that a simple story could express universal truths of human experience. It is for this, as much as anything else, that Spain's greatest work of literature speaks to us as clearly today as it did 400 years ago.

Don Quixote assumes such a dominant role in Spanish literature that it overshadows the works of other Spanish writers. Relatively few other Spanish writers have been translated and widely read in English. One dramatist whose plays are performed regularly outside Spain is Lope de Vega (1562–1635). Lope, as he is known, lived at the same time as Cervantes. Cervantes called Lope "the prodigy of nature," because Lope wrote so much. The universal themes of Lope's plays (honor, justice, and heroism) are always expressed through Spanish settings. His themes and the dramatic quality of his settings are as relevant to audiences everywhere today as they were to Spaniards of the seventeenth century.

Pedro Calderón de la Barca (1600–1681) followed Lope as another world-renowned dramatist of the Siglo de Oro. Calderón was the leading playwright in the royal court of Philip IV. He was associated with the birth of operatic works (*zarzuelas*)

EL INGENIOSO
HIDALGO DON QVI-
XOTE DE LA MANCHA,

Compueſto por *Miguel de Ceruantes*
Saauedra.

DIRIGIDO AL DVQVE DE BEIAR,
Marques de Gibraleon, Conde de Benalcaçar, y Baña-
res, Vizconde de la Puebla de Alcozer, Señor de
las villas de Capilla, Curiel, y
Burguilios.

Año, 1605.

CON PRIVILEGIO,
EN MADRID, Por Iuan de la Cueſta.

Véndeſe en caſa de Franciſco de Robles, librero del Rey nfo ſeñor.

Title page of *Don Quixote*. In 1780, the Spanish Royal Academy reissued a "corrected" four-volume edition of the novel that included a critical introduction, a biography of Cervantes, an analysis of the novel, a chronological survey of Don Quixote's adventures, engravings, and a map of Spain, enabling readers to follow Don Quixote's adventures.

in Spain. He is best known internationally for his play *La vida es sueño* ("Life is a dream"). Calderón remains a great figure in the world of drama for the range and depth of his themes, his understanding of human behavior, and the intelligence of his dramatic craftsmanship.

In 1898, the United States defeated Spain in the Spanish-American War. Spain had to surrender to the United States its ownership of the Philippines and Guam, and give Cuba its independence. Some Spanish writers and philosophers of the time tried to understand the reasons for Spain's long decline, which reached rock bottom with the 1898 defeat. This group came to be known as the Generation of '98 (La generación del '98). They aimed to raise the quality of Spanish literature and philosophical thinking, to pull the country up by its bootstraps, and to restore Spaniards' sense of pride in their country. The leading figures of the Generation of '98 movement were the great philosophical writer Miguel de Unamuno, Azorín (whose real name was José Martínez Ruiz), the socialist writers Pío Baroja and Vicente Blasco Ibáñez, and the great philosopher José Ortega y Gasset.

Pedro Calderón de la Barca was one of Spain's greatest playwrights. In 1637, he was made a knight of the Order of Santiago because of his service to King Philip IV as a writer in the royal court. Toward the end of his life, he wrote mostly religious plays. Calderón's work compares with that of Shakespeare and Molière.

No summary of Spanish literature would be complete without mention of Spain's great twentieth-century poet and playwright Federico García Lorca (1898–1936). Lorca was born in Granada during the Spanish-American War. He became internationally famous for his poetry. He lived in the United States and Cuba in 1929–1930, at the beginning of the Depression. But his true inspiration was the soul of Spain, especially southern Spain, where he was born. Gypsies, bullfighting, folklore, raw human passions, and death were all inspirations for Lorca's poetry, music, and drama. At the age of just thirty-eight, he was murdered by Nationalist soldiers shortly after the start of the Spanish Civil War, bringing him sudden fame around the world. Lorca ranks among the world's great literary figures of the twentieth century.

Portrait of Federico García Lorca. In August 1936, at the beginning of the Spanish Civil War, Franco's Nationalist troops killed Lorca. They believed that intellectuals like Lorca threatened the Nationalist movement. After the Civil War, Lorca was increasingly recognized throughout the world as one of the greatest writers of the twentieth century.

Music and Dance

There are many different kinds of music and dance in Spain. Each region has a speciality. In Galicia people even play the bagpipes. The folk-music tradition in the regions has been preserved in part because modernization came so late to Spain. The influences of European and especially American mass-market culture began to penetrate Spain only toward the end of the Franco dictatorship, in the late 1960s. After that, regional folk culture, including song and dance, began to be overwhelmed by foreign imports. One of the consequences of this "invasion" of outside trends was that regional folk groups emerged in some regions to preserve their traditions. They were often linked to regionalism (by the Basques, Catalans, and Galicians, in particular).

Nowadays, the folk songs and dances of the regions are mainly reserved for special occasions such as fiestas and holidays. The most common music in Spain is the music heard in every country around the world: popular, hard rock, blues, jazz, and every variety in between. Spanish, Catalan, and even Basque popular music is also common. But Spain has evolved as a more European culture since the 1970s. Spaniards travel the world now. There is still popular Spanish music and dance, but international music is even more common.

One kind of regional Spanish music in particular has become famous worldwide: flamenco. The music and dance of flamenco comes from the gypsies of

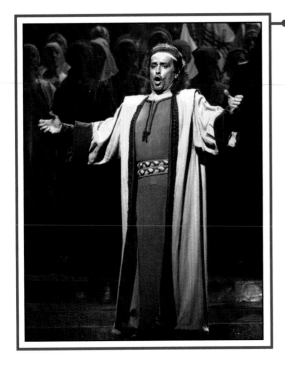

Spanish tenor José Carreras sings during a performance of *Samson et Dalili* in Barcelona. Carreras has performed in many of the world's most important concert and opera houses, including Carnegie Hall in New York, the Royal Albert Hall in London, and Salle Pleyel in Paris.

Andalusia. It started around the fourteenth century. Flamenco was originally spontaneous and improvised. There were no fixed tunes or movements. Now most flamenco music and dancing are well-rehearsed commercial routines. Genuine, spontaneous flamenco is hard to find.

The *cante* (singing) is the basis for flamenco. *Cante jondo* (deep song) is the most serious and deeply moving kind of cante. Flamenco music typically expresses the joys and sorrows (especially the sorrows!) of daily life. The singing is often accompanied by guitar playing. Castanets are also often used now, but they are not part of the original gypsy tradition. The men's dancing in flamenco focuses on rapid toe and heel clicking (*zapateados*), like very quick tap dancing. The women use their hands and bodies in intricate gestures and movements. The soul of flamenco is the *duende*, the spirit of the dance or music that takes over the performer.

There have been well-known classical artists in both music and dance in Spain. The traditional zarzuela (opera) combines song and dance as a lively

Flamenco is Spain's most typical folk music and dance. Combining dance, song, and guitar to express a deep sense of sorrow, flamenco reflects the suffering of gypsies from southern Spain. Flamenco involves improvisation, as dancers perform spontaneously to the music's emotion.

Photograph of Manuel de Falla with Polish harpsichordist Wanda Landowska. De Falla is Spain's most renowned twentieth-century composer. His use of folk music in his work earned him the title of national composer. He supported Franco's Nationalist government until 1938 when he moved to Argentina, where he remained until his death.

and varied spectacle on the stage. It takes its name from the Spanish word for a stew (zarzuela) that has different meat or fish and vegetable ingredients. The greatest Spanish composer of classical music in recent times was Manuel de Falla (1876–1946). One of his first major works was music for the ballet *El amor brujo* ("Love, the magician"). This work is based on traditional Andalusian folk music, raised to a more sophisticated level. De Falla's best-known work is his composition for the ballet *El sombrero de tres picos* ("The three-cornered hat"). All of de Falla's major compositions express the soul of Andalusia, his birthplace.

FAMOUS FOODS AND RECIPES OF SPAIN

9

Spaniards eat a Mediterranean diet. This means lots of fresh fruit and vegetables, lean meat like chicken, fresh fish, olive oil, and not much sweet food like cakes and cookies. The Mediterranean diet is low in fat and sugar and quite high in protein and carbohydrates. This might be why people in Spain live longer, on average, than people in most other countries. The average life expectancy for Spanish men is 75 years, compared with just 72 years for American men. For Spanish women, it is 82 years (79 years for American women). Spaniards also tend to eat less food when they do eat. Until recently, the problem of obesity (being overweight) was very uncommon in Spain. Obesity almost certainly reduces life expectancy. But the way Spaniards eat has changed a lot in the past fifty years.

Spain was a rather poor country until quite recently. People bought the least expensive food they could. The cheapest food was fresh fruit and vegetables, rice, bread, and wine. Meat and fish were luxuries. Sugar and sweet foods like desserts were expensive and were reserved for special occasions. Fortunately, the inexpensive foods were also the healthiest. Women bought fresh produce from the market every day. There were no preservatives. Hardly anyone had a refrigerator or freezer. And since people could not afford much, they ate less, too. Also, until the 1960s, Spain was mainly an agricultural country. Farming employed more people than any other kind of work.

A Spanish family gathers around the table *(left)*. Spaniards typically eat three meals a day. Breakfast is usually coffee and pastries. Lunch might include soup, salad, fish, and fruit. Dinner is usually eaten late, between 9:00 and 11:00 PM. Plates of seafood tapas *(above)*. Eating tapas is a Spanish tradition. Tapas are small dishes, served in bars at any time in between main meals. Many people make an evening of visiting different bars for their varieties of tapas.

A meat vendor in Barcelona. Each region of Spain has its own traditional food. The far north is known for its dishes of beans, sausages, and fish. The northeast coast is best known for its rice-based dishes like paella. The interior of Spain is well known for roast and stewed meat dishes. Fresh produce is available in local markets in all towns and cities in Spain. Supermarkets are also common throughout the country.

Most people spent their workdays doing much more physical labor than they do today. Physical activity burned off fat.

Spaniards still generally have a good basic Mediterranean diet. What has changed is their lifestyle. They have more money to buy different kinds of food. They have less time to cook. Women, who used to spend all day cleaning and cooking, now go out to work. Convenience foods have become part of the modern Spanish lifestyle. Most people have freezers to keep frozen foods and microwave ovens to heat them up. A generation ago, it used to take two hours to make dinner. Now it might take fifteen minutes or half an hour.

Many people think Spanish food is hot and spicy, but it is not. (They confuse it with some Latin American foods that use hot chilies.) Spanish food is simple, down-to-earth, and rustic. Some of the most typical dishes found all around Spain include the *tortilla española*, or Spanish omelette. Other dishes are chorizo (cured sausage), churros (a kind of Spanish deep-fried doughnut), paella (a dish of meat or shellfish and rice flavored with saffron), grilled prawns, and *merluza* (hake, the most common kind of fish). Gazpacho is a cold soup from Andalusia. *Calamares fritos*, or fried squid, is popular. Pork is the most common meat.

Many regions in Spain produce the famous dry-cured hams, *jamón serrano* (mountain ham). The best quality jamón serrano comes from pig-rearing areas in western Andalusia and Extremadura. The hams are the legs of the pig. The leg is first salted down for a few days to draw out the moisture. Then it is washed and hung out to air-dry (cure). Mass-produced hams are hung for a few weeks. The finest quality hams hang for up to eighteen months. The cool, dry mountain air where they are produced is vital to the curing process. The best hams are from free-roaming pigs. Around Jabugo in Andalusia they make jabugo ham from pigs that eat mainly acorns. The acorns give the ham fat a golden color and add a special flavor to the meat. *Jamón ibérico* and *jamón pata negra* are also higher quality than the ordinary jamón serrano. These whole legs of cured ham often hang from the ceilings in Spanish bars. They are very thinly sliced for tapas, or for *bocadillos* (crusty bread sandwiches; *un sandwich* is a sandwich made from sliced white loaf bread.) Cheese is a common filling in bocadillos. There are dozens of different kinds of cheese made in Spain. The best known is Manchego (meaning, "from the region of La Mancha"). Manchego is made from ewe's (sheep's) milk.

Tapas are snacks people get at bars. "Tapa" literally means "lid" or "cover." Its meaning as a bar snack is thought to be from the custom of getting a small plate, with a little snack on top, covering a glass of wine served in a bar. In a bar in Spain, when you get a drink, you are usually also given a small tapa, free. These are usually simple, just a few olives, some potato chips, a few slices of chorizo, nuts, or other tidbits. You can also order your own tapas. There are

Manual harvest of olive trees allows pickers to select the best fruits. A cloth sack is used to collect the olives. Olive growers also use mechanical techniques to shake the olives free from the branches of the trees.

A fish and shellfish market in San Lucar de Barrameda in southwest Spain. With over 1,243 miles (2,000 km) of coastline, seafood is popular throughout Spain. Madrid, at the center of the Iberian Peninsula, is famous for its wharf. Fish and shellfish caught in the Mediterranean and Atlantic are sent overnight to Madrid to satisfy the city's huge demand for seafood.

hundreds of different kinds, at all prices. The most common are *patatas bravas* (spicy potato wedges), *tortilla* (Spanish potato omelette), *croquetas* (croquettes, like dumplings), *ensalada rusa* (potato salad), *boquerones* (anchovy slices, usually pickled in vinegar), *calamares* (squid, deep-fried or sautéed in its own ink), gambas (prawns), and *albóndigas* (meatballs). Tapas range from a simple little plate of salted almonds to a small bowl of stew or a plate of pork chops. Some are more like a meal than a snack!

The different regions of Spain all have different foods. Foods from central Spain are based on meats, beans, and cured sausages. There are dozens of kinds of cured and cooked sausage in Spain (called *embutidos*, collectively). When people had no refrigerators in their homes, cured sausage was the most common way to keep meat. These sausages are mainly made of pork. Others, called *morcilla*, are made from pigs' blood. The most common meat dish in central Spain is *cocido*. This is a stew of meats, sausages, and chickpeas. In Asturias, to the north, the most famous stew is *fabada* (bean stew). This is similar to cocido but uses beans rather than chickpeas. Another dish from the central regions is slow-roasted meat like lamb or kid (small goat). These are slowly roasted for hours in a big stone oven (the *asador*).

In the northwest region of Galicia, fish (*pescado*) and shellfish (*mariscos*) are most common. There is a very special kind of shellfish called *percebes* (goose barnacles) harvested only in Galicia. These ugly long barnacles are attached to the rocks around the coast. Percebes fishermen, called *percebeiros* in Galician, hang down from ropes to pull the percebes off the rocks. It is all done by hand and is very

dangerous work. The sea is often rough. Percebes are the most expensive of all shellfish because they are so difficult to harvest. Another shellfish found only in Galicia is the scallop (*vieira*). These are eaten from their shells, a few at a time. Galicia is also a region of green pastures. Most of Spain's dairy herds are reared here. The best veal in Spain is from Galicia. The most typical Galician dish is the meat or fish pies called *empanadas*. These are shallow pies filled with fish, such as tuna, peppers, onions, and other fillings.

A group of women eat crayfish in Cadiz. Crayfish are a prized delicacy in Spain. The most common fish eaten in Spain is hake (similar to cod). The most unusual is the goose barnacle (percebe), an expensive delicacy from Galicia in the northwest. Meals in Spain still tend to be long and leisurely, although this custom is changing because of busier lifestyles.

Shellfish is delicious and highly appreciated in Spain. There are all kinds of shellfish, from the tiniest prawns to full-grown lobsters (*langostas*). Mussels (*mejillones*) are also very common, especially as a tapa. Squid, either deep-fried or cooked in its ink (*en su tinta*), and octopus (*pulpo*) are also common tapas dishes. Madrileños (people from Madrid) eat more shellfish than almost any other people in Spain, even though Madrid is farther away from the sea than anywhere else in Spain. The people from Cádiz (known as *gaditanos*) in the southwest are also famous shellfish eaters.

A man sells churros, sugary, fried pastries similar to doughnuts. Churros are often eaten with rich, pudding-like hot chocolate. Street vendors cook churros right at their carts. In the United States, churros are made with cinnamon. Spanish churros are usually served with sugar sprinkled on them.

Asturias, on the north coast, has given us its most famous dish, fabada. Grapes do not grow well in this wet part of Spain. The typical drink here is cider (*sidra*) made from locally grown apples. The Basque Country, east of Asturias, is famous for the finest cuisine in Spain and particularly for a fish stew called *marmitako*. The Basque Country is also famous in Spain for its gastronomic societies. These are clubs where men (and only men) gather to cook and eat gourmet dishes. There are hundreds of these clubs all around the Basque Country. They hold regular gourmet cooking and eating evenings, as well as competitions. It's no surprise that some of the best restaurants in Spain are in this region.

On the Mediterranean coast, the food of Catalonia is the most diverse in all of Spain. There is fish and shellfish, but also chicken, rabbit, local sausages (*butifarras*), and Spain's sparkling wine (*cava*) region just to the south of Barcelona. Catalan cooking probably uses more different kinds of ingredients than any other region of Spain. There is a whole cuisine from Catalonia. In most other parts of Spain, there are just various regional specialities.

The Valencia region has given the world the most traditional Spanish dish of all: paella. The Romans introduced irrigation in the area around Valencia. The invading Moors later introduced rice (which is grown in irrigated, water-logged paddies). Centuries later, rice became the staple local food. Now Valencia is the rice capital of Spain, and paella is its most famous rice-based food. The name paella originally referred to the pan it was cooked in: *a paellera* (from the Latin word for a cooking pan, *patella*). There is no one way to make paella. Everyone has his or her own recipe. Originally it was made with snails that were common in the Valencian wetlands. Now it tends to be made with chicken, rabbit, or seafood, or combinations of those ingredients, and rice. The most important ingredient for making paella is short-grain rice.

Paella

Ingredients (Serves 8)

¼ cup olive oil (or enough to cover the base of the cooking pan)
2 cups 1- to 2-inch cubes of chicken (or other white meat such as rabbit or turkey), seasoned
2 to 3 cloves garlic, minced
1 large onion, diced
4¼ cups boiling chicken stock
2 teaspoons saffron (preferably the stems, not powdered)
1 red pepper, sliced
1 green pepper, sliced
½ cup fresh parsley, chopped
2 cups medium-grain rice (such as arborio)
1 cup peas, cooked
chorizo sausage, sliced*
belly pork, seasoned and cubed*
shrimp, mussels in shells, and/or clams, cooked*
(* optional)

Procedure

Heat the olive oil in pan. Fry the chicken pieces until well browned. If using other raw meats, fry these, too.

Transfer the cooked chicken and other meat to a plate. Reduce heat and cook garlic gently for a few minutes. Remove garlic from pan to a mortar and pestle. Fry onion gently until soft.

Meanwhile, in the mortar and pestle, pound together a little hot stock with the saffron, garlic, and about half the parsley, to get a rough pulpy blend (called the *majado*). When the onion is soft and just translucent, add sliced red and green peppers. Cook gently until soft, about five minutes. Stir in the rice. Cook gently for a few more minutes, stirring to coat the rice well with the oil in the pan. Add the hot stock and majado. The saffron in the majado will turn the rice a light yellow.

Boil rapidly for 8 to 10 minutes. Reduce the heat to moderate or low. Simmer for 8 to 10 minutes more.

Test a few grains of rice for doneness. It should be cooked through, but still firm (al dente). Turn off the heat when the rice is done. Let the rice stand for several minutes.

To finish the paella, stir in the cooked peas and optional ingredients such as chorizo and/or previously cooked mussels, shrimp, and/or clams. Sprinkle the rest of the parsley over the paella. Cover the paella with a clean cloth or lid to let it steam a few minutes before serving.

Saffron is the spice that gives paella its subtle flavor and yellow color.

Paella

The original paella from the Valencia region used snails as a main ingredient with the locally grown round-grain rice. It was cooked in the field over an open fire. Snails rarely appear nowadays in paella, and the dish is usually cooked on a kitchen stove. Everyone has his or her own way of making paella, but it is important to use the right rice (a round, medium-size grain, such as arborio used in risotto), real saffron, and, if possible, an authentic paella pan (the paellero). You can substitute a wide, deep cooking pan or casserole pot with a thick stainless-steel base if you don't have the genuine paellero.

It is also important not to stir the rice in the final ten to fifteen minutes of cooking, so as not to break the rice grains and make them mushy.

A food store in Toledo. Spanish food was influenced by imports from the New World. Today many dishes include tomato, potato, vanilla, chocolate, and zucchini, which were originally native to the Americas. Spanish cooking is characterized by simple preparation and fresh ingredients.

Flan, a popular Spanish dessert, can be found ready-made in supermarkets. A type of caramel-topped custard, it is baked and turned out of its mold. Many traditional Spanish desserts feature egg yolks as the main ingredient.

A crust should form on the bottom of the rice, the sign of a well-cooked paella.

Probably the most widely eaten food from Spain is the olive (*aceituna* or *oliva*) and olive oil (*aceite de oliva*). Spain is the world's biggest producer of olive oil. Most of it comes from the south, but olives are grown all around the country. Some of the finest olive oil comes from Catalonia. The olives not used to make olive oil are sold as ordinary olives for eating. Spain, one of the main sources of fresh vegetables exported to other European countries in the winter months, is also one of the world's biggest producers of wine. The best-quality Spanish wines are made in the Rioja region in the northeast. Sherry and the finest Spanish brandy are made around Jerez de la Frontera in the southwest. Jerez, or Xérès in the local dialect, is the origin of the English word "sherry."

The most common dessert in Spain is flan. A custard or crème caramel, it is served cold in the little pot it's cooked in. In times past, the sherry producers in southern Spain clarified (purified) the sherry with large amounts of egg white. That left a lot of egg yolks to use in some other way. Thus, egg yolks (without the whites) are the basic ingredient for flan. In Catalonia, people have their own version of flan called *crema catalana*, which is virtually the same as the French "burnt custard" dessert crème brulée.

Another sweet Spanish delicacy that has become internationally known is turrón, or nougat. The turrón-making capital of Spain is around Alicante, on the southeast Mediterranean coast. Turrón is made in thick slabs, like chocolate bars. A hard, brittle version of turrón is made around the town of Alicante. A soft version is made nearby, at Jijona.

DAILY LIFE AND CUSTOMS IN SPAIN

10

I t used to be said that *España es diferente* ("Spain is different"). This meant that it was cut off from the rest of Europe. It was isolated. It was less developed. It was distinctively *diferente*. Franco's dictatorship kept Spain behind the rest of Europe. He prohibited liberal influences such as democracy, a free press, freedom of speech, and long hair. After he died, there was an explosion of freedoms in Spain. Once prohibited by Franco, hundreds of political parties emerged. The press, media, and entertainment, which had all been censored by Franco, suddenly went wild. It took ten years after Franco's death for the country to settle down. Then, in 1986, Spain joined the European Economic Community (now called the European Union). From that time on, *España* became less and less *diferente*. Spaniards wanted a higher, European standard of living. They wanted new things, more money, and greater freedoms. They no longer wanted to be *españoles* (Spanish) like their parents' generation. They wanted to be European españoles, like their children.

So, now Spain is still distinctive. But it is much less different than it used to be. The art and architecture, the popular traditions, fiestas and customs, and the languages of Spain are all still there. What has changed remarkably in the last generation are the

A woman works in a coal mine in Figaredo *(left)*. Women constitute one-third of Spain's workforce. Along with working outside the home, women are still generally expected to care for the children and maintain the household. Men relax on a bench in Aragon *(above)*. Spanish people have a strong sense of personal pride and individuality. They value modesty rather than assertiveness. Spaniards regard personal appearance, image, and strong relationships with family and friends as important elements in their daily lives.

People shop at a market in Majorca. In Spain, people tend to dress more conservatively than in the United States. Men dress more formally in muted colors. Women typically appreciate styling and simplicity. Name brand clothing is important.

lifestyles and aspirations of the Spaniards themselves. The country was closed off from the rest of the world for so long. Now it is among the most open and liberal societies of Europe. The standard of living of Spaniards is getting closer to the European average. (The average annual income of Spaniards is approximately one-third less than the European Union average. It is about half the American average.)

One of the most noticeable things about Spain today is that people have cars, washing machines, television sets, microwave ovens, satellite TVs, and other modern conveniences. A generation ago they were lucky to have a refrigerator. In 1960 only about 5 percent of Spaniards had televisions. Now they have more than one, on average, per household. The first big item that Spaniards typically buy (apart from a home) is a car. Today Spain's cities are badly congested with cars, motorbikes, and buses. The only time of the day when the streets are quiet is between 2:00 and 4:00 PM: lunchtime.

Eating times are still the one big difference between Spain and other countries. Breakfast is at a typical time, around 7:00 to 8:00 AM. But lunch isn't until around 2:00 or even 3:00 PM. So most people go out to a nearby bar or café for a late morning coffee and snack. The lunch period (it could hardly be called a lunch hour!) is from 2:00 to 4:00 or even 5:00 PM. A late-afternoon break from work might include a *merienda* (snack) with tea or coffee. Most people work until 7:00 or 8:00 PM. (Government offices, however, usually close at 2:00 PM.) After work, people might stop at a bar or café for a drink and tapas. Dinner is anytime between 9:00 and 11:00 PM. It might be even later on weekends.

People meet to drink, eat tapas, and socialize mostly outside the home. They get together in bars, cafés, and cafeterias for a mid-morning break, a drink and tapas before lunch or dinner, and well into the night after dinner. The small bars where people meet to socialize are called *tascas*. They often have TV sets permanently

turned on in the corner, jukeboxes, and basic slot machines. (Spaniards gamble an average of $650 per person a year!) Many people smoke: Spaniards smoke more than any other people in Europe except the Greeks. Smoking is declining now, as it is regarded as a health hazard. However, it is still a very common custom to offer someone a cigarette as a friendly gesture.

Famously, Spaniards take a siesta (nap) during the afternoon lunch break. In fact, the siesta is dying out. The lunch break is still long, because lunches are often three-course family meals. Even with the many fast-food chains in Spain now, the long lunch period has survived. But family lunch at home during the week is becoming less common, especially in the bigger towns and cities. Also, there are many foreign companies in Spain. Their working hours are like working hours elsewhere in the world. As a result, Spaniards spend less time at lunch at home and more time having a "working lunch" in the office. The traffic, too, gives commuters little time to have a siesta after lunch. Now they have to get back in their cars to fight the traffic back to work.

Diners at the Plaza Mayor in Madrid. The Plaza Mayor is located where Arab merchants once had a marketplace, just outside the walls of Madrid's old city. During the sixteenth century, Philip II ordered the run-down marketplace to be cleared and a square (plaza) to be constructed in its place. The square would serve as a showplace as well as a center for commerce and social life. Today, the Plaza Mayor is a center of social activity in the heart of Madrid.

After work, from around 7:00 to 9:00 PM, Spaniards still take time for the traditional evening paseo (stroll). Groups of families and friends walk up and down the sidewalks of the town or around the square. They stop to shop or just window-shop. The bars and cafés fill up with people drinking and eating tapas. (There's even a verb in Spanish, *tapear*, that means to go around different bars eating tapas.) In winter, when the weather is often below freezing, Spaniards still go out for their ritual paseo. In summer, after the heat of the day, it is even more popular. During the midday lunch break, the streets are usually deserted.

Dinner is usually anytime after about 9:00 PM. In the south it tends to be even later. Foreign tourists are usually the only people in Spanish restaurants before 9:00 PM! It is not at all unusual to eat dinner at 10:00 PM and then go to a movie afterward! For most families, however, dinner usually takes place in front of the TV. All eyes are glued to a popular program. Spaniards watch more television, on average, than almost any other Europeans—about three and a half hours a day. (Only the British, among all Europeans, watch more TV.)

Dinner at 11:00 PM or even after midnight is not unusual, especially on weekends. Madrileños (people from Madrid) might stay out until 3:00 or 4:00 in the morning on Friday or Saturday nights. Discotheques and nightclubs in the big cities might stay open until 6:00 AM. The biggest traffic jams in Madrid are at 3:00 or 4:00 on Saturday and Sunday mornings! It's not surprising that there's a verb in Spanish that means being up and about in the early hours of the morning (*madrugar*; the *madrugada* is "early morning"). More often than not, this means still being up and about, rather than just getting up for breakfast.

In Spanish, you greet people according to the Spanish time of day. For example, "Buenos días"

Retiro Park, the big central park of Madrid. The park offers 350 acres of paths, lakes, and gardens. Retiro Park was originally the garden of the Palace of the Buen Retiro. It was opened to the public in 1868. Popular amongst Madrileños (people from Madrid) and tourists alike, the park is especially well-used on weekends.

("Good morning") goes from the time you wake up until about lunchtime. Then it becomes "Buenas tardes" ("Good afternoon" or "evening"). This lasts more or less until it's time for bed. The meaning of "Buenas noches" ("Good night") is more like, "Well, it's two in the morning, guys, and I'm late for dinner, so, buenas noches!"

Weekends are for family life in Spain. People tend to wake up quite late. They might go for a paseo for a few hours around midday. Public parks are crowded. A swim at the local public pool or a few games of tennis at the public courts are also popular. The big family meal takes place around 3:00 PM. There's usually a soccer game on television on Sundays. Or friends to visit. Or a movie to see. In the summer, there are sidewalk cafés (*terrazas*) to sit at and drink and eat. Sunday night, before the working week starts, is an early night: bed by around midnight!

Shopping used to be done every day. Most food was bought fresh from the local produce markets. Nowadays most people shop in supermarkets. There are still local markets for fresh foods, but the supermarket has become the most convenient way to shop. There are also hypermarkets (*hipermercados*). These are very big stores that sell food, appliances, clothes, and other household items. Most of the hypermarkets are at the center of big shopping malls, surrounded by smaller specialty stores.

The biggest spectator sport in Spain by far is *fútbol* (soccer). The season goes from September to June. There are four professional divisions. The biggest clubs in the Primera División (First Division), such as Real Madrid and Barcelona, have fans all around the

A vendor in the Basque region sells sardines. The fish are usually eaten grilled. Spaniards eat more seafood than almost any other group in Europe. As well as fish, Spaniards eat octopus, squid, mussels, and several kinds of crayfish. In some places, sea urchins are a speciality.

Soccer *(fútbol)* is the most popular sport in Spain, with many soccer leagues throughout the country. The most important is the Golden League, which has teams in all major towns and cities. The different climates and landscapes of the country provide for a variety of outdoor activities. Hiking, rock climbing, horseback riding, fishing, and skiing are all popular leisure activities in Spain.

world. The home stadiums of Real Madrid (the Bernabeu) and Barcelona (the Nou Camp) are almost as famous as the clubs themselves. All the big First Division league games are broadcast on television and radio. Bars with television sets fill up with spectators whenever there is a game on between a local club and a traditional rival. (Real Madrid versus Barcelona games are broadcast worldwide.) Basketball is the second most popular professional sport in Spain. There are no separate divisions, just eighteen individual teams in a single league (the Liga ACB). Cycling and tennis are also big sports in Spain. The success of golfers such as Seve Ballesteros, José María Olazábal, and Sergio García has boosted the popularity of golf.

After soccer, bullfighting attracts the second highest number of spectators as a public spectacle. Its popularity is greatest in the south, the central regions, and in some parts of the north. In Catalonia, bullfighting is not popular among Catalans. Bullfighting attracts fans in Catalonia mainly because of the large number of Andalusian immigrants there from the south. It is also a popular tourist spectacle. In

Government-run lotteries, casino gambling, football pools, horse racing, bingo, and slot machines are very popular in Spain. The biggest national lottery is run by ONCE, the Spanish national association for the blind. ONCE's big Christmas lottery is known as *el gordo* (the fat one). Thirty percent of lottery revenues are allocated to the national treasury.

the Canary Islands, bullfighting has been banned.

August is vacation month in Spain. Many people take the whole month off work. More people nowadays take just two weeks off, but summer working hours are often shorter. Many offices close early so people can enjoy the afternoon and evening. Stores and tourist sites are among the few places that stay open the whole month. The most popular destination for vacations within Spain is the Mediterranean coast. Around 20 percent of all Spaniards vacationing within Spain go to Andalusia. Apart from August, the other main tourist season is Easter and Holy Week. Spaniards travel outside Spain more, as they become more affluent. They go mainly to other Spanish-speaking places such as Cuba, the Dominican Republic, and the countries of Latin America. However, other countries in Europe are very popular, too. Spanish is among the most common languages heard in European cities these days.

EDUCATION AND WORK IN SPAIN

In the years before and just after the Spanish Civil War (1936–1939), Spain was a very poor country. Many people, especially in rural areas, were illiterate (*analfabetos*, in Spanish; *analfabetismo* is "illiteracy" in Spanish). The generation born after the Spanish Civil War had a great desire to improve their standard of living and level of education. (One of the worst insults in Spanish is to call someone *mal educado* or *inculto*, both meaning, basically, "ignorant.") As a result,

education became very important for people from the 1960s onward. There was a huge increase in the number of students at universities in particular. In 1960, there were only around 75,000 students at Spanish universities. By 1990, there were around 1.2 million. Now there are 1.5 million university students. Students can study for as long as they want until they pass the final exams. The average time taken to get a university degree varies between about eight years for five-year courses and six years for three-year courses.

In the academic year of 2001 to 2002, there were 8.3 million students in all levels of education in Spain: 1.2 million were in infant schools, 2.5 million were in primary schools (six to twelve years old), 1.9 million were

A winemaker shows off his grape harvest *(left)*. Wine growers rely on the Church as much as on good weather to ensure a good grape harvest. A symbolic bunch of grapes is blessed before the harvest, and a thanksgiving service is held at the conclusion of the harvest season. After the grapes are harvested, winemakers crush and ferment the grapes to make wine. Approximately 500 grapes are needed for one bottle of wine. College students study outside *(above)*. Spain's higher education is provided mainly by public institutions.

in secondary schools (twelve to sixteen years old), 720,000 were in the pre-university two-year *bachillerato* diploma courses (sixteen to eighteen years old), 1.5 million attended university, and just fewer than 500,000 were in professional (vocational) training courses. Just less than 90 percent of the school and university age population of Spain is being formally educated. Young people are becoming much better educated than their parents and grandparents were. The general level of education of the population overall, however, is still low compared to other countries. Only about 25 percent of the population in the twenty-five- to sixty-four-year-old age group have completed secondary education. In the United States, 80 percent of that age group has had secondary school education. The level is low in Spain because of the older generations whose education was not as good as that of young people today.

Improving educational standards has been a priority for the government since the 1980s. Education up to the age of sixteen has been compulsory since the passing of a new education reform law in 1990. Before that, education was required up to the age of fourteen. Basic public education to the age of sixteen is free.

Primary school education lasts six years, from ages six to twelve years old. Secondary education lasts four years, from ages twelve to sixteen. Students can then go on to do two years of what is called the bachillerato, two years of higher studies before university. Alternatively, they can do the two-year *formación profesional* (professional training) diploma course. This is for more practical, less academic (vocational)

subjects. At the end of the two-year bachillerato or formación profesional, students take exams. They have to pass all their exams to get the diploma. If they then want to go on to university,

Students in an art class at a school in Madrid. Spain's education system requires schools to offer religious instruction, although attendance is voluntary. A liberal arts education is mandatory. Students are required to attend school until they are fifteen years old.

they take university entrance exams. There are sixty-seven universities in Spain: forty-eight are public, and nineteen are private. Almost half of all university students study law or social science courses. Less than 10 percent study science courses such as medicine. The result is that Spanish universities produce huge numbers of graduates in law or other general studies. They produce relatively few graduates in professional areas such as medicine and engineering.

The oldest university in Spain is at Salamanca, founded in 1218, when the Moors were still occupying southern Spain. The largest university in Spain is Universidad Nacional de Educación a Distancia (National University for Distance Learning), abbreviated to UNED. Around 135,000 students are enrolled at UNED. Teaching is done through correspondence and multimedia such as radio, television, video, and the Internet. The Complutense University of Madrid is the largest conventional university in Spain. It has about 100,000 students. There are also a number of postgraduate business schools that offer higher degrees (mainly the master of business administration, or MBA). Getting an MBA in Spain today is a great advantage in finding a high-paying job with a big company.

Work

In the years before the Spanish Civil War, most people in Spain worked on the land in agriculture. Agriculture now employs only about 6 percent of the working population. More than 60 percent of the working population is employed in service industries such as tourism, banking and financial services, the legal profession, accounting and consulting,

Fishermen pack their nets after returning with an early morning catch in Salobreña. The fishing industry in Spain accounts for $330 million of the economy. Employing nearly 28,000 people, Spain's fishing fleet is one of the largest in the world.

and what are called the distributive trades (retail and wholesale businesses). About 20 percent is employed in manufacturing industries (the auto industry, steel making, chemicals, shipbuilding, and so on). Another 10 to 12 percent work in the construction industry. Unemployment in Spain has been very high over the past twenty years: from 15 to 20 percent, compared with 3 to 5 percent in the United States.

Most companies in Spain today are still small businesses that employ fewer than 100 people. Many foreign companies set up factories in Spain years ago to take advantage of low costs, especially the low salaries they paid employees. Ford and General Motors, for example, have been making cars in Spain since the early years of the twentieth century. The whole Spanish car industry, in fact, is now owned entirely by foreign (American, other European, and Japanese) companies. Most of the biggest information technology (IT) companies are foreign owned: Hewlett-Packard, IBM, Fujitsu, and so on. The biggest electronic appliances companies, such as Sony, Philips, and Electrolux, all have Spanish subsidiaries (secondary companies). Many large multinational companies are among Spain's 100 biggest companies. Spain no longer has the low costs that attracted such companies in the past. It still has a lot of potential growth, however. Spain also has modern technology, a well-educated labor force, reasonable living costs, and seaports on both the Mediterranean and Atlantic coasts to ship exports.

The best-known Spanish companies are probably its food and drinks producers. Chupa Chups, for example, is famous all over the world for its lollipops. Freixenet and Codorníu are Spain's biggest producers of sparkling wine. They export all over the world, too. And there are numerous Spanish wine (including sherry) and brandy producers well known in many countries. One of the biggest names in Spanish fashion, Adolfo Domínguez, is almost as well known in New York or London as it is in Madrid and Barcelona. By far the biggest export companies are the car producers. They sell more cars in other European countries than they sell within Spain.

Women used to be confined mainly to the home in Spanish society. Laws from the Franco dictatorship discriminated against women. Since the late 1960s, more women have gotten higher education (secondary schools and universities). The 1978 Constitution declared that sexual discrimination was illegal. The number of

Chupa Chups' production factory in Barcelona makes gourmet lollipops. Chupa Chups sells 4 billion lollipops a year, in 40 flavors and in 170 countries. Concocted in Spain in the early 1950s, these lollipops are among the best-selling candies in the world. Their logo was designed in 1969 by Spanish surrealist artist Salvador Dali. Many famous people, such as Madonna, Elton John, Brandy, Sheryl Crow, and Magic Johnson, have promoted Chupa Chups lollipops.

In Madrid, there's always time to have a shine put on your shoes. In 1999, a labor integration program promoted the profession of *limpiabota*, or shoe shiner. In Catalonia, the local government provided small subsidies for the limpiabotas.

women in the workplace increased, as did the status of women. Nowadays women hold positions of power, especially in public service (as judges, government ministers, mayors, and ambassadors). They are a much greater part of the workforce than they used to be. Even so, not many women hold positions of power in private companies. That is still largely male territory.

One reason for this is the *enchufe* (plug-in) system in Spain. To be *enchufado* means to be "plugged in." It means having friends or relatives who help one another with favors: getting a job, a loan, a contract, or an advantage of one kind or another. Everything, of course, is informal and unofficial. A handshake or a word in someone's ear and the wheels are set in motion. And it's reciprocal—both sides benefit. Women, for the most part, are not part of the male-oriented enchufe system. This has made it difficult for them to rise up the company ladder. Enchufe oils the wheels of business life. You can go far in Spain if you're "plugged in" with the right connections.

Generally people's working hours in Spain are from 9:00 AM to 2:00 PM and from 4:00 PM to 6:00 or 7:00 PM. Government and other public service employees usually stop work at 2:00 PM. Big companies often have a canteen for coffee breaks and lunch. Otherwise people usually go home for lunch. Bringing a paper bag with sandwiches to have lunch in the office is rare in Spain. Nowadays, however, especially in the bigger cities, more people have a quick lunch at a fast-food outlet or cafeteria. There are hundreds of American fast-food restaurants, as well as some Spanish chains that offer more typical Spanish foods. Some workers also use cafeterias that offer a daily set lunch of three courses. These are usually self-service restaurants. Many of them accept payment in luncheon vouchers (vouchers of a fixed value given by companies to employees as part of their employment terms).

Traffic congestion in the big cities makes it impractical for many people to travel half an hour to their suburban home for lunch and half an hour back to work.

The work culture in Spain has become more and more international. People travel out of Spain on business trips. Salaries are getting to be as high as in other European countries. Vacation time in Spain (four weeks a year) is much like other places in the rest of Europe. Tourism has brought many outside influences into Spain, including the way people dress, their attitudes and behavior, and their affluence. A few generations ago Spaniards worked in order to survive. Now they work for job satisfaction and to enjoy their leisure time. Work has become a way of achieving goals and dreams rather than just a way to put food on the table. As much as anything else, this difference reflects the Spain of today and tomorrow, compared with the Spain of generations past.

Vacationers sunbathe on the beaches of Majorca. Mass-market tourism to Spain began in the 1960s. Spain now attracts more foreign visitors than its total population: about 50 million people in 2002. Income from foreign tourism is $35–40 billion a year. The industry currently employs about 10 percent of the Spanish workforce, although tourism jobs in many areas are seasonal and therefore temporary.

SPAIN
AT A GLANCE

HISTORY

The first signs of human habitation in Spain were the neolithic cave paintings dating from 15,000 to 20,000 years ago. The first inhabitants were the Iberian tribes from around this time. They left some examples of writing, but the meaning of these writings remains a mystery. People from other Mediterranean civilizations arrived from about 800 BC: Phoenicians, Greeks, Carthaginians, and Romans.

In the year 409, Gothic tribes (Vandals, Suebians, Alans) began to invade Spain. In 456 the Visigoths, another Germanic tribe, invaded. Within ten years they overthrew Roman rule in Spain. Over the next centuries, the various tribes in Spain feuded and struggled for power. Moorish forces from North Africa invaded in 711. There followed almost 800 years of Islamic occupation. This was also the period of the so-called Reconquest of Spain by Christian forces, a period of constant warring between Moors and Christians. Southern Spain was dominated mainly by Moorish kingdoms. Islamic influences took root in architecture, literature, and the Spanish language (Castilian Spanish). The Christian kingdoms of Castile and Aragon dominated the central heartland and north of Spain.

The Moors were finally confined to a single kingdom, Granada. In 1492, they were conquered and driven out of Spain. In the same year, the Jews were expelled from Spain by the Catholic monarchs Ferdinand and Isabella. In September that same year, Christopher Columbus set foot in the New World. The marriage of Ferdinand, king of Aragon, and Isabella, queen of Castile, in 1469, had started the process of uniting the kingdoms of Castile and Aragon. Their union led to the creation of Spain as a single nation under one monarch. Over the following centuries, Spain became a European state. Its rulers brought periods of peace and prosperity, as well as war and depression.

In 1898, Spain suffered a disastrous defeat in the Spanish-American War. It lost its overseas possessions (Cuba, the Philippines, and Puerto Rico) to the United States. In 1923, a general, Miguel Primo de Rivera (1870–1930), overthrew the government in a coup d'état. His dictatorship (the First Republic) lasted until he was forced out of office in January of 1930. An alliance of Republicans and Socialists won the elections in 1931. The king, Alfonso XIII, abdicated (gave up the throne) and left Spain.

Between 1931 and 1936 (the Second Republic), various political parties ruled Spain. It was a period of great instability and conflict. José Antonio Primo de Rivera (1903–1936), the eldest son of the dictator Miguel Primo de Rivera, founded the right-wing Spanish Falangist party in 1933. The Spanish Civil War began in 1936 with a military revolt against the government. Nationalists (the military) fought against Republicans (government forces) for three years. The war left hundreds of thousands dead. There was terrible suffering for all Spaniards. Victory went to the Nationalists on April 1, 1939. One of the generals who led the military revolt in 1936, Francisco Franco, became dictator.

For almost forty years, Franco ruled Spain with an iron fist. A few days after Franco's death in 1975, the heir to the throne, Juan Carlos, was crowned king. Spain began its transition toward democracy. In 1978, a new constitution was approved by popular vote. Among other things, it guaranteed Spanish citizens equal human, social, and political rights, which Franco had for so long denied them. In 1986, Spain became a member of the European Economic Community (now the European Union). Spain has since evolved into a modern, democratic, and liberal society of equal standing among its European neighbors.

ECONOMY

The Spanish economy was a mess after the Spanish Civil War. Franco tried to fix the economy by giving financial aid to industry and by introducing high import duties to protect Spanish industries against imports. He created a massive state-owned holding company, Instituto Nacional de Industria (INI), to build up Spanish industry. INI companies were subsidized (financially supported) by the state. They were Spain's biggest producers of iron and steel, coal, electricity, ships, refined oil products, chemicals, and many other heavy industrial products. Most INI companies made huge losses which the state absorbed.

The result of Franco's industrialization program in the 1950s was high inflation and a disastrous government deficit, meaning more money was spent than earned. Inflation was so high it reduced salaries to lower than they were before the Spanish Civil War, in the 1930s. In 1959, Franco was forced to introduce the so-called Stabilization Plan. The plan halved the value of the currency (the peseta). This made it cheap for foreign tourists to visit Spain: They got twice as many pesetas for their own currency as before. There was also a boom in foreign investment since labor costs were still very low.

The economy started to pick up. In the 1960s, economic growth in Spain was higher than in any other European country. Income from tourism rose from just $130 million in 1960 to about $1 billion by 1965. Around this time, too, many Spaniards left Spain to work in other European countries. More than 1 million emigrated in the years between 1960 and 1973. In that period they sent back about $5 billion to the families they had left in Spain. Tourism, foreign investment, and money from emigrant Spaniards fuelled Spain's growth in the 1960s.

In 1973, however, the price of oil on the world market skyrocketed. The higher price of oil in 1973 and again in 1978 sent Spain's economy into recession until 1982. (Spain has to import all the oil and most of the gas it uses for energy.) From the mid-1980s, there was a new wave of growth. Foreign investment and tourism increased.

In 1986, Spain joined the European Economic Community (EEC), now called the European Union. From that time it gradually adapted to EEC legislation to make the Spanish economy more competitive. State subsidies had to be abolished. The huge state-owned INI companies were sold to private owners (a process called privatization). Since 1986, all the INI companies have gradually been privatized. Franco protected certain sectors of industry by creating single state-owned companies that had no competition. These monopolies were also broken up by the late 1990s. In that same time, many banks and private companies merged to form bigger companies, to become more powerful. It remains to be seen whether, by becoming bigger, they have also become more profitable and competitive. Even the biggest Spanish companies are rather small by comparison with big companies in other European countries.

Early in 2002 the Spanish currency, the peseta, was replaced by the European Union currency, the euro. Spain's economy is now geared to the economy of the greater European Union. Most of the regional governments in Spain are enthusiastic supporters of regionalism within the larger European Union. In less than thirty years, Spain has gone from the repressive, isolationist regime of Franco's dictatorship to full integration with the European Union. The future of Spain—its economy, its regions, its people—is now intimately related to the evolution of that union.

GOVERNMENT AND POLITICS

Spain is a parliamentary monarchy, with a democratically elected Parliament and a hereditary monarch. King Juan Carlos is head of state. Since the elections of May 1996, the prime minister has been José María Aznar, head of the Partido Popular (Popular Party, or PP). The Spanish Parliament (las Cortes) has two chambers: a senate (Senado) and the Congress of Deputies (Congreso de Deputados). There are 208 members of the Senate elected by popular vote and 51 are appointed by regional governments. All serve four-year terms. The 350 members of Congress are elected by popular vote to four-year terms. Elections were held in March 2000. Aznar's party, the PP, is conservative. Its main competitor, the Partido Socialista Obrero Español (Spanish Socialist Workers Party, or PSOE), is Socialist. Regional parties, such as Convergencia i Unió from Catalonia and Partido Nacional Vasco from the Basque Country, are important minority parties in Parliament.

Spain is a country of distinctive regions. Today there are eighteen administrative regions called the Comunidades Autónomas (Autonomous Regions). They are similar to the states of the United States, except that each one has a different contract with the central government of Madrid. This means that each region governs its affairs independent from the other regions, according to the terms it has agreed upon with the central government of Madrid. The regions all have standard institutions such as a prime minister, parliament, and courts. The regional government of Catalonia, called the Generalitat, has existed since 1359. It has the most independence of any regional government.

The eighteen Comunidades Autónomas are Andalusia, Aragon, Asturias, the Balearic Islands, Basque Country, the Canary Islands, Cantabria, Castile–La Mancha, Castile-León, Catalonia, Extremadura, Galicia, La Rioja, Madrid, Murcia, Navarra, Valencia, and the North African territories of Ceuta and Melilla (combined as one).

Distributed among the regions (excluding Ceuta and Melilla) are fifty provinces. These have their own administrative powers, including some functions delegated directly by the central government. There are more than 8,000 municipal authorities. They are represented in the *ayuntamientos* (town halls) of Spain's cities, towns, and villages. The head of the municipal council (*pleno*) is the mayor (*alcalde*). The ayuntamientos are responsible for basic public services. The extent of their responsibilities depends on the population of the municipality.

TIMELINE

30,000–20,000 BC

First settlers, Iberians, populate Iberian Peninsula.

16,000 BC

First cave paintings made in northern Spain.

218 BC

Romans invade Spain.

800 BC

Carthaginians establish city of Cádiz in southern Spain.

AD 409

Invasion by tribes of Suebians, Vandals, and Alans ends Roman domination.

1478

Inquisition established.

1479

Castile and Aragon unite, the first step toward unified Spain.

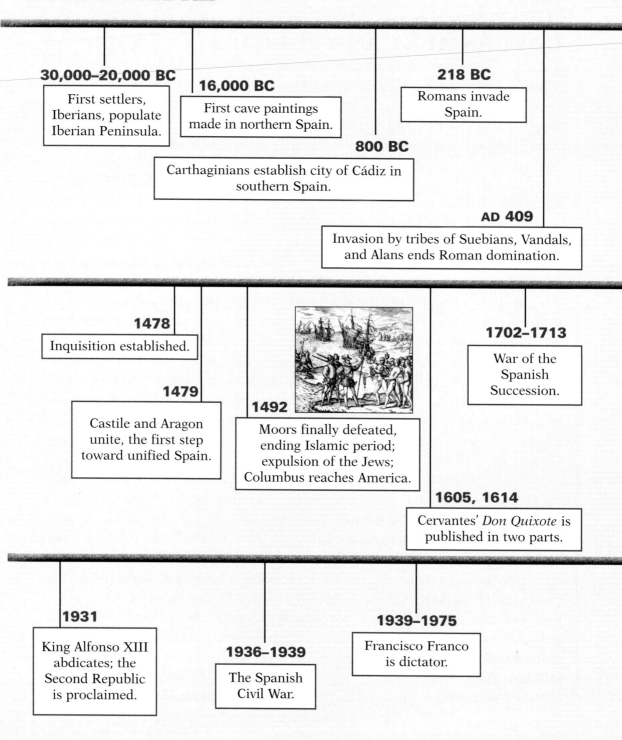

1492

Moors finally defeated, ending Islamic period; expulsion of the Jews; Columbus reaches America.

1702–1713

War of the Spanish Succession.

1605, 1614

Cervantes' *Don Quixote* is published in two parts.

1931

King Alfonso XIII abdicates; the Second Republic is proclaimed.

1936–1939

The Spanish Civil War.

1939–1975

Francisco Franco is dictator.

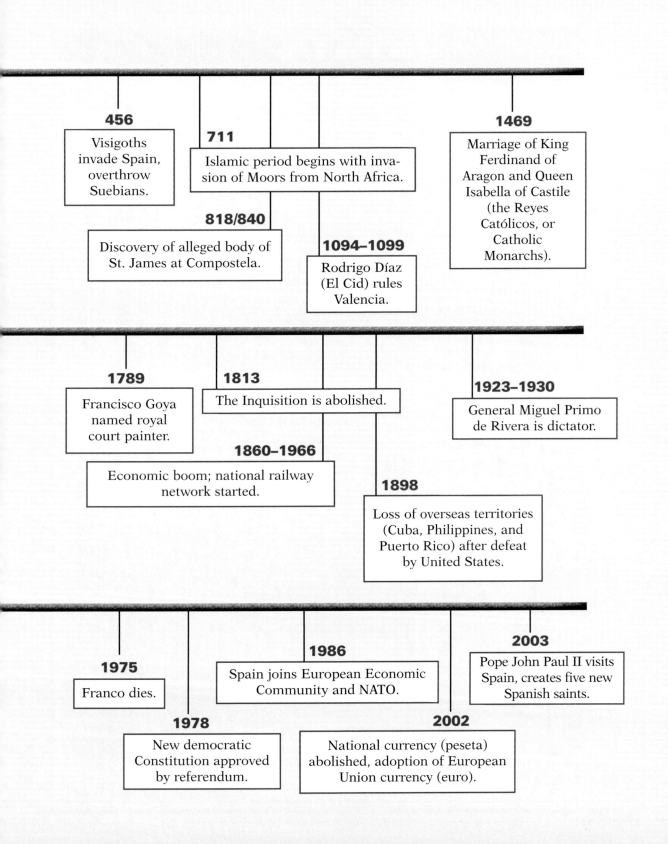

456
Visigoths invade Spain, overthrow Suebians.

711
Islamic period begins with invasion of Moors from North Africa.

818/840
Discovery of alleged body of St. James at Compostela.

1094–1099
Rodrigo Díaz (El Cid) rules Valencia.

1469
Marriage of King Ferdinand of Aragon and Queen Isabella of Castile (the Reyes Católicos, or Catholic Monarchs).

1789
Francisco Goya named royal court painter.

1813
The Inquisition is abolished.

1923–1930
General Miguel Primo de Rivera is dictator.

1860–1966
Economic boom; national railway network started.

1898
Loss of overseas territories (Cuba, Philippines, and Puerto Rico) after defeat by United States.

1975
Franco dies.

1986
Spain joins European Economic Community and NATO.

2003
Pope John Paul II visits Spain, creates five new Spanish saints.

1978
New democratic Constitution approved by referendum.

2002
National currency (peseta) abolished, adoption of European Union currency (euro).

SPAIN

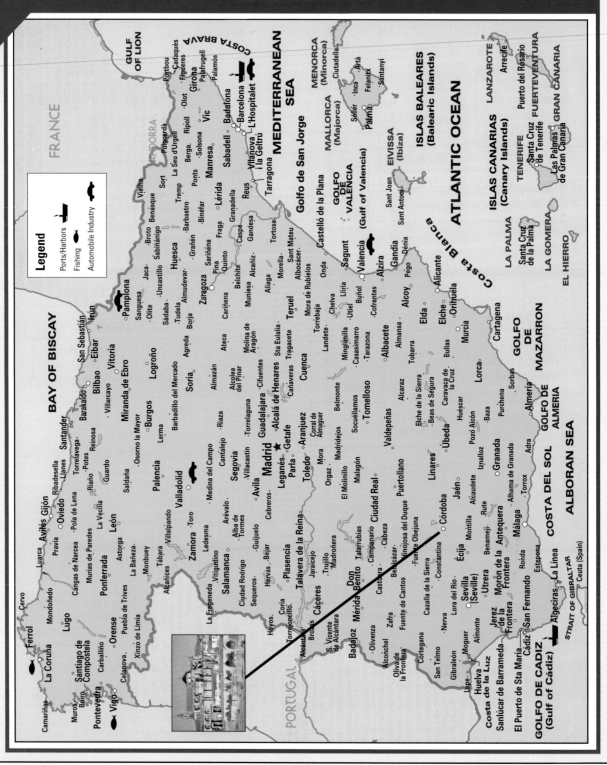

GULF OF LION

COSTA BRAVA

FRANCE

ANDORRA

Portbou
Cadaqués
Figueres
Palafrugell
Girona
Palamós

MEDITERRANEAN SEA

MENORCA (Minorca)
Ciutadella
Artá
Inca
Santanyí
Felanitx

ISLAS BALEARES (Balearic Islands)

MALLORCA (Majorca)
Sóller
Palma

EIVISSA (Ibiza)
Sant Joan
Sant Antoni

ATLANTIC OCEAN

ISLAS CANARIAS (Canary Islands)

LANZAROTE
Arrecife

FUERTEVENTURA
Puerto del Rosario

TENERIFE
Santa Cruz de Tenerife

GRAN CANARIA
Las Palmas de Gran Canaria

LA PALMA
Santa Cruz de la Palma

LA GOMERA

EL HIERRO

Puigcerdá
La Seu d'Urgell
Ripoll
Olot
Vic
Berga
Solsona
Manresa
Sabadell
Badalona
Barcelona
L'Hospitalet
Vilanova i la Geltrú
Tarragona
Reus
Lérida
Ponts
Sort
Tremp
Vielha

Golfo de San Jorge

GOLFO DE VALENCIA (Gulf of Valencia)

Castelló de la Plana

Sagunt
Valencia
Alzira
Gandia
Dénia
Pego
Alicante
Orihuela
Elche

Costa Blanca

GOLFO DE MAZARRON

Cartagena
Murcia

Jaca
Uncastillo
Broto
Sabiñánigo
Graus
Benasque
La Puebla de...
Barbastro
Huesca
Binéfar
Fraga
Almudevar
Graién
Sariñena
Pina
Quinto
Caspe
Gandesa
Sant Mateu
Morella
Aliaga
Alcañiz
Muniesa
Belchite
Cariñena
Zaragoza
Sádaba
Tudela
Borja
Ágreda
Tarazona

Sangüesa
Olite
Pamplona
Irún
San Sebastián
Eibar
Vitoria
Bilbao
Barakaldo
Miranda de Ebro
Logroño
Soria
Almazán
Alcolea del Pinar
Cifuentes
Molina de Aragón
Teruel
Mora de Rubielos
Landete
Chelva
Liria
Buñol
Utiel
Cofrentes
Alcoy
Elda
Almansa
Alcira

BAY OF BISCAY

Santander
Torrelavega
Reinosa
Potes
Riaño
Guardo
Saldaña
Osorno la Mayor
Lerma
Burgos
Palencia
Valladolid
Medina del Campo
Cantalejo
Riaza
Torrelaguna
Segovia
Guadalajara
Alcalá de Henares
Cuenca
Cañaveras
Tragacete
Belmonte
Minglanilla
Casasimarro
Tarazona
Alcaraz
Albacete
Tobarra
Bullas
Lorca
Sorbas
Purchena
Baza
Huéscar
Beas de Segura
Caravaca de la Cruz
Elche de la Sierra

Luarca
Avilés
Gijón
Oviedo
Pola de Lena
La Vecilla
León
Villarcayo
Barbadillo del Mercado
Ledesma
Cebreros
Ávila
Orgaz
Mora
Madridejos
Socuéllamos
Tomelloso
Valdepeñas
Alcázar...
Pozo Alcón
Úbeda
Linares

Ribadesella
Llanes
Cangas de Narcea
Murias de Paredes
Ponferrada
Astorga
La Bañeza
Villalpando
Zamora
Toro
Arévalo
Alba de Tormes
Guijuelo
Salamanca
Ciudad Rodrigo
Sequeros
Plasencia
Talavera de la Reina
Madridejos
El Molinillo
Malagón
Ciudad Real
Puertollano
Jaén
Alcaudete
Iznalloz
Granada
Alhama de Granada
Torrox
Adra
Almería

Mondoñedo
Lugo
Cervo
Ferrol
La Coruña
Santiago de Compostela
Carballino
Pontevedra
Orense
Xinzo de Limia
Celanova
Vigo
Camariñas
Muros
Boiro

Monbuey
Tábara
Alcañices
La Fregeneda
Vitigudino
Hervás
Béjar
Coria
Torrejoncillo
Hoyos
Brozas
Alcántara
S. Vicente de Alcántara
Badajoz
Mérida
Don Benito
Cáceres
Trujillo
Madroñera
Talarrubias
Campanario
Castuera
Cabeza...
Hinojosa del Duque
Belalcázar
Fuente Obejuna
Constantina
Peñarroya
Córdoba
Montilla
Rute
Benameji
Morón de la Frontera
Antequera
Ronda
Estepona
Málaga

PORTUGAL

Madrid
Leganés
Getafe
Parla
Aranjuez
Toledo

Olivenza
Alconchel
Olivo de la Frontera
Zafra
Fuente de Cantos
Cortegana
San Telmo
Gibraleón
Lepe
Moguer
Almonte
Huelva
Costa de la Luz
Sanlúcar de Barrameda
El Puerto de Sta María
Cádiz
San Fernando
Jerez de la Frontera
Utrera
Lora del Río
Sevilla (Seville)
Nerva
Cazalla de la Sierra
Jaraicejo

GOLFO DE CADIZ (Gulf of Cádiz)

COSTA DEL SOL

ALBORAN SEA

GOLFO DE ALMERIA

La Línea
Algeciras
STRAIT OF GIBRALTAR
Ceuta (Spain)

Legend

Ports/Harbors

Fishing

Automobile Industry

ECONOMIC FACT SHEET

GDP in US dollars: $720.8 billion (2000 estimate)

GDP Sectors: Services 65%, industry 30%, agriculture 5%

Land Use: Cropland 37%; grassland, grazing, forests 46%; other 13%

Currency: Euro (from May 2003) $1 = 1.1932 euro

Workforce: 17 million

Major Agricultural Products: Cereals, beef and pork products, fresh fruits, olives, vegetables, and wine

Major Exports: Automobiles, chemicals, footwear, fruits and vegetables, fuel and refined oil products, industrial machinery, iron and steel products, and plastic products

Major Imports: Automobiles, chemicals, electrical machinery, fish and shellfish, fuels and refined oil products, industrial machinery, iron and steel products, optical and photographic equipment, plastic products, pharmaceuticals

Significant Trading Partners (2001):

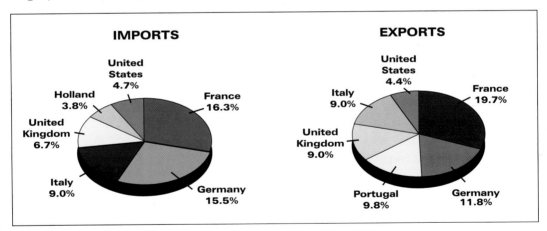

Rate of Unemployment: 13% (2001)

Highways: 216,786 miles (346,858 km)

Railroads: 8,719 miles (13,950 km)

Waterways: 653 miles (1,045 km)

Airports: 35

POLITICAL FACT SHEET

Official Country Name: Kingdom of Spain (usually just called Spain, España)

Capital: Madrid

Official Flag: Two horizontal red bands on top and bottom, double-width yellow horizontal band in middle; national coat of arms on the hoist side showing royal seal framed

by the Pillars of Hercules (the two points, one in Spain and the other in Morocco, on either side of the Strait of Gibraltar)

Government: Head of state: King Juan Carlos; prime minister: José María Aznar. Parliament: two chambers, Senate (259 members, of which 208 elected by popular vote and 51 appointed by regional governments) and Congress of Deputies (350 members elected by popular vote). Cabinet: Council of Ministers appointed by prime minister. Regions: eighteen Comunidades Autónomas with own regional government administrations. Constitution: December 1978.

Voting age: 18

Election: Every four years

Number of Registered Voters: In the 2000 national elections, there were 33,969,640 registered voters, of which 23,339,490 (68.5%) voted.

National Anthem: One of the oldest in Europe, "La Marcha Real" (The Royal March) is one of the few national anthems which has a tune, but no words. It was composed in 1761. During the rule of Franco (1939–1975) lyrics were written by José María Pemán, but they never became official.

CULTURAL FACT SHEET

Official Language: Castilian Spanish

Unofficial Languages: Catalan, Basque, Galician

Major Religions: 99% Catholic, less than 1% other

Capital: Madrid

Population: 40.2 million; Men: 19.7 million; women: 20.5 million

Ethnic Groups: Mediterranean/Nordic Caucasian (est. 99%); approximately 1 million foreign nationals resident in Spain

Life Expectancy: Men: 75.5 years; women: 82.5 years

Time: Greenwich Mean Time (GMT) + 1 hour

Literacy Rate: 97%

Cultural Leaders:
> **Visual Arts:** Diego de Velázquez, Francisco de Goya, Bartolomé Esteban Murillo, Francisco de Zurburán, Pablo Picasso, Joan Mirò, Salvador Dalí
> **Literature:** Miguel de Cervantes, Lope de Vega, Pío Baroja, Miguel de Unamuno y Jugo, Federico García Lorca
> **Music/Dance:** Manuel de Falla, Plácido Domingo, Carlos Montoya (flamenco), Andrés Segovia

National Holidays and Festivals

New Year's Day: January 1

Good Friday: Friday before Easter

Labor Day/May Day: May 1

Assumption of the Virgin Mary: August 15

National Day: October 12

All Saints' Day: November 1

Spanish Constitution Day: December 6

Christmas Day: December 25

Working Life: Since 1983, forty hours has been the length of the official legal maximum work week in Spain. Bargaining agreements between companies and trade unions usually reduce this to a thirty-six- to thirty-eight-hour work week. In addition to having time off on weekends and public holidays, workers officially have thirty days of paid holiday a year. Collective bargaining agreements often result in workers gaining an additional five days of vacation, which is called the "fifth week."

GLOSSARY

arid (AYR-id) Dry or parched.

autonomous (aw-TONN-oh-mus) Independent, self governing.

density (DEN-seh-tee) The condition of being closely packed together; thickness or compactness.

dictator (DIK-tay-ter) One who exercises supreme authority in a country, usually without having been elected to do so.

dominant (DAH-mih-nent) In charge.

expel (ex-PELL) To drive out.

fertile (FER-tul) Good for making and growing things.

heretic (HEHR-eh-tik) A person whose religious beliefs are different from those of the accepted church.

Inquisition (in-quih-ZI-shun) Roman Catholic tribunal established in the fifteenth century for the discovery, examination, and trial of heretics

irrigate (EAR-ih-gayt) To supply land with water through ditches or pipes.

papier-mâché (PAY-per-mah-SHAY) Paper mixed with water to make a paste that can be molded when wet. When it dries, it becomes hard and strong.

plateau (plat-TOW) An elevated, relatively flat area of land.

population density (pop-yoo-LAY-shun DEN-sih-tee) The total number of people living in a certain place.

FOR MORE INFORMATION

Embassy of Spain in Canada
74 Stanley Avenue
Ottawa, ON K1M 1P4
(613) 747-2252/7293
e-mail: embespca@mail.mae.es
Web site: http://www.docuweb.ca/
    SpainInCanada

Embassy of Spain in the United States
2375 Pennsylvania Avenue NW
Washington, DC 20037
(202) 452-6100
Web site: http://www.spainemb.org/ingles/
    indexing.htm

Spanish National Tourist Office in
 Los Angeles
San Vicente Plaza Building
8383 Willshire Blvd., Suite 960
Beverly Hills, CA 90211
(213) 658-7188
e-mail: losangeles@tourspain.es
Jurisdiction: Washington, Oregon,
 California, Nevada, Montana, Idaho,
 Wyoming, Utah, Colorado, Arizona,
 New Mexico, Alaska, and Hawaii

Spanish National Tourist Office
 in Chicago
845 North Michigan Avenue, Suite 915
Chicago, IL 60611
(312) 642-1992
e-mail: chicago@tourspain.es
Jurisdiction: Ohio, Michigan, Indiana,
 Illinois, Wisconsin, Minnesota,
 Iowa, Kansas, Oklahoma, Nebraska,
 North Dakota, South Dakota, and
 Missouri

Spanish National Tourist Office in Miami
1221 Brickell Avenue, Suite 1850
Miami, FL 33131
(305) 358-1992
e-mail: miami@tourspain.es
Jurisdiction: Texas, Arkansas,
 Louisiana, Mississippi,Tennessee,
 Kentucky, North Carolina, South
 Carolina, Georgia, Alabama, Florida,
 and insular states in the Caribbean

Spanish National Tourist Office
 in New York
666 Fifth Avenue, Suite 35
New York, NY 10103
(212) 265-8822
(888) 657-7246
e-mail: ontny@tourspain.es
Jurisdiction: Maine, New Hampshire,
 Vermont, Massachusetts, Rhode
 Island, Connecticut, New York, New
 Jersey, Pennsylvania, Delaware, West
 Virginia, Maryland, Virginia, and
 Washington, DC

Web Sites

Due to the changing nature of Internet
links, the Rosen Publishing Group, Inc.,
has developed an online list of Web sites
related to the subject of this book. This
site is updated regularly. Please use this
link to access the list:

http://www.rosenlinks.com/pswc/spai

FOR FURTHER READING

Barlow, Genevieve, and William Stivers. *Stories from Spain/Historias de España* (Side-by-Side Bi-lingual). Chicago: Passport Books, 1999.

Butcher, N. *The Spanish Kitchen.* London: Macmillan, 1990.

Casa, Penelope. *The Foods and Wines of Spain.* New York: Alfred A. Knopf, 1982.

Smolan, Rick, and David Cohen. *A Day in the Life of Spain.* San Francisco: Collins Publishing, 1987.

Spence, Lewis. *Spain—Myths and Legends.* London: Senate/Studio Editions, 1994.

BIBLIOGRAPHY

Carr, Raymond, ed. *Spain—A History.* Oxford, UK: Oxford University Press, 2000.

Crow, John A. *The Roots and the Flower.* Berkley, CA: University of California Press, 1985.

Gies, David T. *The Cambridge Companion to Modern Spanish Culture.* Cambridge University Press: Cambridge, UK, 1999.

Hooper, John. *The New Spaniards.* New York: Penguin Books, 1995.

Rodgers, Eamonn, ed. *Encyclopedia of Contemporary Spanish Culture.* London/New York: Routledge, 1999.

Williams, Mark. *The Story of Spain.* Santana Books: Malaga, Spain, 2000.

PRIMARY SOURCE IMAGE LIST

Page 20: Mesolithic stone lance head located at the Museu d'Arqueologia de Catalunya in Barcelona, Spain.

Page 22: Altamira cave painting, located in northern Spain, created by the Magdalenian culture and dating from between 16,000 and 9,000 BC.

Page 24: Iberian sculpture dating from between the fourth and second centuries BC.

Page 25 (top): A sarcophagus dates from between the fifth and first centuries BC and is located in the National Archaeological Museum in Beirut, Lebanon.

Page 27: Fresco of the conquest of Majorca was painted by an unknown Arab and dates circa AD 1229. It is housed at the Museu Nacional d'Art de Catalunya in Barcelona, Spain.

Page 28 (top): A fresco depicting the conquest of Majorca shows the city's fortifications. It dates from 1229 and is housed at the Museu Nacional d'Art de Catalunya in Barcelona, Spain.

Page 28 (bottom): Fifteenth-century dish with Arabic inscription.

Page 29: *The Surrender of Granada* by Francisco Ortiz Pradilla was completed between 1879 and 1882 and is located at the Capilla Real in Granada, Spain.

Page 30 (top): A painting of Queen Isabella and King Ferdinand dates from 1469.

Page 30 (bottom): A woodcut of the Visigoths capturing Rome was created circa 1486. It is located at the Bibliothèque Nationale de France in Paris, France.

Page 31 (top): Oil on canvas portrait of Charles V, painted by Jacob Seisenegger in 1532. It is located at the Kunsthistorisches Museum in Vienna, Austria.

Page 31 (bottom): Map by Juan de la Cosa, dates from AD 1500 and is located at the Museo Naval de Madrid in Madrid, Spain.

Page 32 (top): Photograph taken in 1936 of Republican fighters surrendering.

Page 32 (bottom): Photograph of General Franco.

Page 37: Poster advertising a bullfight in Cadiz is dated June 8, 1885.

Page 41: Illustration titled *Open-Air Feast* dates from 1554 and is housed at the Biblioteca Monasterio del Escorial in Madrid, Spain.

Page 48: Illumination from the *Chronicles of Spain*, which was written in the fourteenth century.

Page 49: Illustration of the Battle of Roncesvalles.

Page 50: Reproduction of a map of Santiago de Compostela. The original was engraved by D. Serveaux in 1648.

Page 51: Reproduction of Roland blowing his horn at the Battle of Roncesvalles. The original is from an original manuscript of *Le Chanson de Roland*, which dates from the thirteenth century and is located at Saint-Gall in Switzerland.

Page 60: Stone relief depicts the compulsory baptism of Moorish women at the conquest of Granada. It was created by Felipe Vigarny de Borgona circa 1520 and is located at the Royal Chapel of the Cathedral of Granada in Granada, Spain.

Page 61: Portrait of Saint Ignatius of Loyola is from *Gallery of Portraits* published in 1833.

Page 62: Construction of the Mezquita was completed in AD 786 in Córdoba, Spain.

Page 64: Illustration of an auto-da-fé dates from 1692 and appeared in Philip of Limborch's *Historia Inquisitionis*.

Page 66: A nineteenth-century engraving of Ferdinand VII swearing in the constitution in the Salon de Cortés.

Page 69: Oil on canvas painting by Diego Rodriguez Velazquez completed in 1656. It is located at the Museo Prado in Madrid, Spain.

Page 70: Lady of Elche statue dates from the fourth century BC and is housed at the National Archeological Museum in Madrid, Spain.

Page 72: The Alhambra dates from 1238 and is located in Granada, Spain.

Page 74: Oil on canvas painting titled *Burial of the Count of Orgaz* by El Greco dates from 1588 and is located in the Church of Santo Tomé in Toledo, Spain.

Page 75: Sketch titled *Barbarians* is part of Francisco de Goya's series *Disasters of War*, completed between 1808 and 1814. It is now located at the Bibliothèque Nationale de France in Paris, France.

Page 76 (bottom): The oil on canvas painting *The Persistence of Memory* is by Salvador Dalí. It was painted in 1931 and is located at the Museum of Modern Art in New York City.

Page 78: A nineteenth-century oil on canvas painting appeared in an edition of Miguel de Cervantes' novel *Don Quixote*. It is now housed at Caylus Anticuario in Madrid, Spain.

Page 81: First edition title page of *Don Quixote* by Miguel de Cervantes, published in Madrid in 1605.

Page 82: Portrait of Pedro Calderón de la Barca.

Page 83: Portrait of Federico García Lorca by Gregorio Toledo.

Page 85: Photo of Manuel de Falla and Wanda Landowska, taken in Granada, Spain, in 1930.

INDEX

About the Author

Graham Faiella published a monthly business report about Spain for twelve years. He now writes nonfiction books, mainly on subjects related to the sea. He is originally from Bermuda and has lived in the United Kingdom since 1974.

Designer: Geri Fletcher; **Cover Designer:** Tahara Hasan; **Editor:** Jill Jarnow;
Photo Researcher: Gillian Harper; **Photo Research Assistant:** Fernanda Rocha